THE
HOLY
SPIRIT

**Other Abingdon Press Books by Stanley Hauerwas
and William H. Willimon**

*Resident Aliens: Life in the Christian Colony (Expanded
25th Anniversary Edition)*
Where Resident Aliens Live: Exercises for Christian Practice
The Truth about God: The Ten Commandments in Christian Life
Lord, Teach Us: The Lord's Prayer and the Christian Life

THE HOLY

STANLEY HAUERWAS
WILLIAM H. WILLIMON

SPIRIT

Abingdon Press
Nashville

THE HOLY SPIRIT

This book is printed on acid-free paper.

Library of Congress Cataloging-in-Publication Data

Hauerwas, Stanley, 1940–
  The Holy Spirit / Stanley Hauerwas, William H. Willimon. — First [edition].
    pages cm
  Includes bibliographical references.
  ISBN 978-1-4267-7863-6 (binding: soft back) 1. Holy Spirit. I. Title.
  BT121.3.H38 2015
  231'.3—dc23

                                                                      2015016800

15 16 17 18 19 20 21 22 23 24—10 9 8 7 6 5 4 3 2 1
MANUFACTURED IN THE UNITED STATES OF AMERICA

To those who, by the Holy Spirit, are our pastors
Clarke French
and
Heather Rodrigues

CONTENTS

INTRODUCTION

C hristians are nothing without the Holy Spirit. The historic core of the service of ordination is the *Veni Creator Spiritus*, "Come, Creator Spirit." The church in its wisdom knows that pastoral leadership, preaching, and care ought not be attempted alone. Just as the Spirit brooded over the waters at creation, the church is birthed by the Holy Spirit. The church lives not by savvy, worldly wisdom, and techniques for church growth but rather lives moment by moment, in every time and place, utterly dependent upon the gifts of the Spirit. Thus the Holy Spirit is nothing less than a life-and-death matter for the people of God.

Christians are people who dare to live in the power of the Holy Spirit, that is, live lives out of control, coming to God dependent, empty-handed, lives driven by and accountable to someone more interesting than ourselves.

You will note a number of themes recur in our exploration of the Spirit: When we talk about the Holy Spirit, we are talking about God, who is one as Father, Son, and Holy Spirit. The Holy Spirit is more than a personal experience; the Holy Spirit is who God is and what God does as the Trinity, whether we feel it or not. Because the Holy Spirit is intensely communitarian, relational, and embodied, we have the church. Whatever we say about the Holy Spirit must be tested by and congruent with the life, death, and resurrection of Jesus. The Holy Spirit is that gift whereby even in a world at war, we may live in peace, our enemies can become friends, and even in a culture of lies, we can tell the truth. "Come, Holy Spirit!" is the first and last prayer of the church, our only hope in life and death. In receiving the gift of the Holy Spirit, we can begin the adventure of discipleship and end all our attempts at self-justification. Holiness is the fruit of the Spirit and a sure test of holiness is love.

"COME, HOLY SPIRIT!" IS THE FIRST AND LAST PRAYER OF THE CHURCH.

Jesus commands us to venture courageous, countercultural, demanding lives. He orders us to love one another, to pray for our enemies, to take up the cross and follow. But he does not expect us to do these demanding tasks or to live and to die by ourselves. Christ gives us what we need to be as holy as he calls us to be. Thus the church prays for the gift of the Holy Spirit (*Epiclesis*) every time we read scripture, preach, celebrate the Eucharist, or stand against injustice. We know that we cannot pray as we ought, enjoy the peace of Christ, or be the body of Christ in motion except through the gifts of the Spirit. Little in the Christian faith is self-derived.

Therefore we write this book as a practice of prayer, bold to believe that little in our celebration of the Holy Spirit is original with us. A quarter of a century ago, we coauthored *Resident Aliens: Life in the Christian Colony*.[1] This book is therefore a demonstration of how two friends have, under the influence of the Holy Spirit, continued to grow in their faith. Even as this book is a collaborative effort, we'll try to think with our friends the saints, for the church, and under the influence of the Holy Spirit. That these words might be helpful to fellow Christians and to a church facing new challenges, that you and your church may hear these words of ours as God's address to you, God's summons, blessing, and disruption, we pray, "Come, Holy Spirit!"

Chapter One

TRINITY

When we talk about the Holy Spirit, we are talking about God. You may find this an odd remark with which to begin a book meant to introduce the doctrine of the Holy Spirit. After all, this is a book written by Christians for Christians. However, throughout Christian history, and particularly in our own day, Christians have had difficulty remembering that when they say *Holy Spirit*, they're saying *God*.

God as Father, Son, and . . .

Surveys show that nine out of ten Americans say they believe in God. But we're not sure that the God in whom so many Americans believe is the God designated by "Holy Spirit." Actually, when Christians say *Holy Spirit*, they are not merely saying *God*; they are saying *Trinity*: Father, Son, and Holy Spirit, who are the one God. The Holy Spirit is the third person of the Trinity. Often when you are third in a list, for instance, a list like the Apostles' Creed, it can seem that third is an afterthought.[1]

Thus the general presumption is that the Father creates, the Son redeems, and the Spirit—well, what does the Spirit do? Too often the Spirit is associated with our feeling that we have had some sort of "experience" that is somehow associated with God or at least a vague feeling that seems to be "spiritual." Human experience is a questionable place from which to begin thinking about God. Scripture, tradition, reason, and experience are often cited by United Methodists as constituting authority in theological argument. Some even claim that John Wesley was big on experience as a source for theological reflection. Subjective experience is no place to begin thinking about the Holy Spirit. Such thinking can result in a dismissal of what the Bible says about the Holy Spirit and an unfortunate degradation of Christian doctrine. So we say again: To believe in the Holy Spirit is to believe in God. *To have had an experience of the Holy Spirit is to have had an experience of something other than yourself.*

WHEN WE TALK ABOUT THE HOLY SPIRIT, WE ARE TALKING ABOUT GOD.

The question of the status of the Son and the Holy Spirit was the subject of the Council of Nicaea (325 CE). In order to achieve unity of the empire, Constantine ordered the bishops of the church to agree on how best to understand God. The bishops would then become the agents of the empire, ensuring all worshipped the same God. How was the emperor to hold the empire together if there was disagreement about what was real, that is, who was God?

Nicaea faced a big problem: A number of Christians, generally known as followers of Arius, emphasized the uniqueness and transcendence of the Father. Arians taught that nothing could be as special as God, so the Son and the Holy Spirit were not of the same "substance" as the Father. There must have been a time when the Son and the Holy Spirit did not exist. In other words they believed that the Son and the Spirit were subordinate, later creations of the creator. They did not believe that all the members of Trinity were equal; Son and Holy Spirit were God, but not quite.

Their views on God meant that Arians were hard-pressed to explain why Christians had from the first worshipped and prayed to Jesus. The first martyr, Stephen, as he was dying, prayed to Jesus, rather remarkable for a faithful Jew who believed that there was one and only one God who ought to be worshipped (Acts 7). If Christians prayed to Jesus, his identity as God could not be denied. So the early debates surrounding the Trinity were arguments about the status of Jesus. If Jesus was fully God *and* fully human, then some account had to be given of Jesus's relationship to the Father. Nicaea was the church's response to that fundamental challenge. At Nicaea Arius's position (that Jesus was somehow God, but in a derivative, subordinate way) was rejected. Jesus was affirmed as being of "the same substance" as the Father and, therefore, rightly prayed to as the second person of the Trinity.

3

Nicaea kept the Christian view of Christ as complicated as it needed to be to do justice to the New Testament witness. Christ is fully human *and* fully divine, fully divine *and* fully human. When we say the Apostles' Creed, one might think that after we have said, "I believe in God the Father Almighty, maker of heaven and earth," we might have said all we need to say about God. After all, something like nine out of ten Americans seem to believe that God designates the one who is creator. But in the creed we continue, "*and* I believe in Jesus Christ," "*and* I believe in the Holy Spirit." Most heresies are attempts to simplify belief about God. Orthodox Christian theology keeps our thought about God as complex as it needs to be in order to be faithful to the one God who is triune.

Nicaea affirmed not only Jesus as the second person of the Trinity but also the Spirit as the third person of the Trinity. But, as H. E. W. Turner observes, once the Nicene faith had provided some scaffolding to respond to the problem of how the Christian God could be both one and three, "the elaboration of the doctrine of the Holy Spirit followed as a doctrinal 'rider.'"[2] Turner's judgment is confirmed by developments after Nicaea that were primarily concerned with Christology. That is, the challenge was to understand how Jesus could at once be fully God yet fully human. The later Council of Chalcedon (451), which confirmed that Jesus was at once fully God and fully man, was mostly a debate about Christ.

That Christology was so central for Christian theology has led some to charge that because of Nicaea *the Holy Spirit has been given short shrift in the theology of the Christian West.* Augustine is often regarded as the origin of the Western tradition. Augustine allegedly emphasized the unity of the three persons of the Trinity in a manner that made it difficult to know the distinct role of each person of the Trinity. Though the Western theologians did not deny that the Holy Spirit has a role in the Christian life, the emphasis has been more on the work of the Son in obedience to the Father and less about the Holy Spirit as one in being and action with the Father and the Son.

THE HOLY SPIRIT HAS BEEN GIVEN SHORT SHRIFT IN THE THEOLOGY OF THE CHRISTIAN WEST.

Recent theological developments, particularly the theology of Karl Barth, have helped recover for the Western church the significance of the Trinity. The trouble with this renewed reclaiming of the significance of the Trinity is much like what happened at Nicaea. The recovery has been so centered on Christ some theologians have asked, "Is there nothing the Spirit can do that the Son can't do better?"[3] For example, Gene Rogers observes in the second article of the Nicene Creed that we are given a story about the Son that attracts our attention much more than what almost appears to be the random list that follows our affirmation of the Holy Spirit.

In the second article we list some of the extraordinary events associated with Jesus's person and work. We affirm that Jesus is the only Son of God, begotten not made; through him all things were made. He came down from heaven, became incarnate in the virgin Mary, was crucified under Pontius Pilate, suffered death only to be raised on the third day, and ascended to heaven to sit at the right hand of the Father. Moreover he is said to come again to judge the living and the dead.

The Spirit, who was mentioned as having a role in Mary's conception of Jesus, does not enjoy such a dramatic narrative in the Apostles' or Nicene Creeds. Why does our belief in "the holy catholic church" come right after our belief in the Holy Spirit? The Apostles' and Nicene Creeds give the impression that Jesus has a more interesting history than the Holy Spirit. Yet isolation of the Spirit from the Son is a mistake. One of the fundamental tasks of the Holy Spirit is to rest on the Son. *Pneumatology*, the name of the theological specialization dealing with the Holy Spirit, and *Christology*, the theology of the person and work of Christ, are interrelated, making any attempt to treat one without the other a breeding ground for heresies that say too much or too little for the Holy Spirit.

Pentecostal Embarrassment

The Holy Spirit's lack of prominence in contemporary theology is odd given that the movement generally known as *Pentecostalism* is the fastest-growing form of Christianity. *Charismatic* Christianity has grown exponentially over the last century. The movement that many think began in 1906 in modest circumstances on Azusa Street in Los Angeles has exploded into a worldwide phenomenon, producing some of the liveliest churches in South America and Africa.

Of particular note is the Holy Spirit's special relation with the poor and the dispossessed. The sermon that Jesus preached in Luke 4, claiming that the Spirit was upon him to preach good news to the oppressed and deliverance to prisoners, is taking form in worldwide Pentecostalism today.

The charismatic, Holy Spirit–induced movement has not been restricted to Protestants. In 1967 during a retreat at Duquesne University, a number of the participants were "reborn" in the Spirit. It was not long before the movement spread to the University of Notre Dame, spawning summer meetings that attracted thousands. This Catholic charismatic movement has generally had the support of the popes and bishops.

Charismatic forms of Protestantism have often received a different response from the churches. In fact, the "enthusiasm" of the charismatics may be one of the reasons the Holy Spirit does not have, at least among mainstream Protestants, the same status as Father and Son. *Enthusiasm* (infused with God) was a frequent charge against John Wesley and his Methodists.

Some fundamentalist churches ostracize members who claim to have received charismatic gifts, seeing such claims as dangerous, undercutting the authority of scripture, and disrupting congregational order. As mainstream Protestantism loses the social and political status it once enjoyed and is unable to attract new members, it becomes fearful about the future. Mainline Protestants sense that just identifying themselves as Christian is enough of a threat to secular culture; they are anxious not to be counted with Christians who speak in tongues, perform signs and wonders, believe in miracles, and are possessed by the Spirit. Progressive Christians know that many of their secular friends think that Christianity can no longer be rationally defended. That some Christians in the name of the Holy Spirit claim to be possessed by God in a way that seems irrational to modern, Western people only reinforces the secularist suspicion of the absurdity of Christianity.

THE "ENTHUSIASM" OF THE CHARISMATICS MAY BE ONE OF THE REASONS THE HOLY SPIRIT DOES NOT HAVE, AT LEAST AMONG MAINSTREAM PROTESTANTS, THE SAME STATUS AS FATHER AND SON.

In a field education seminar, Will had a student present a case study in which a parishioner asked her pastor, "What does The United Methodist Church believe about speaking in tongues?"

The pastor was rather pleased with himself to respond, "Oh my God, don't tell me you've gotten into that!"

She reported that she had experienced *glossolalia*, ecstatic speech, during a session of her Bible study group.

"Perhaps you are still dealing with grief over the death of your daughter," said the pastor.

"I am. Is that what causes this?" she asked.

"Perhaps you ought to seek professional help," persisted the pastor.

"That's why I came to you," she concluded.

We find this a rather brutal policing of the Holy Spirit to assume that a report of unusual spiritual gifts should be responded to with "You are insane."

Another reason why the Holy Spirit has not been prominent in contemporary theology is that some have used the Spirit to bolster their claim that they have a relationship with God that is peculiar to them alone. Appeals to the Holy Spirit are thus sometimes used to give authority to the individual consciousness that implies that the person making the appeal to "the Spirit" assumes he or she has license to make Christianity up, acting as if his or her experience with God is not dependent on the church. Some even claim to have a special relationship with God through the Holy Spirit but do not think the god to whom they are related is the Trinity. There are charismatic Christians who have conveyed the attitude of "I have the gift of the Holy Spirit. You don't; therefore I'm superior in my faith."

Most churches need some Pentecostal, charismatic Christians present to keep the body supple, moving, and lively; most Pentecostal, charismatic Christians need to be in the body of Christ, the church, to keep themselves in a spirit of embodied love.

That's why *we must begin by thinking about the Trinity if we are to think rightly about and (more important) pray to the Holy Spirit.* Most doctrines of the church, like the doctrine of the Trinity, are the result of controversy. Christians usually only know what they believe when someone has gotten it wrong. That is why those who come to be called *heretics* (like the Arians) are among the blessed. Christians achieved greater clarity about how the God we worship is one being but three persons because some Christians thought the Son and the Spirit were not fully God.

While trinitarian reflections on the Holy Spirit do not say everything that needs to be said about the Holy Spirit, everything that needs to be said about the Holy Spirit must be disciplined by trinitarian convictions. All the Holy Spirit's work is done as the third person of the Trinity: God the Holy Spirit working in concert with God the Father and God the Son.

WE MUST BEGIN BY THINKING ABOUT THE TRINITY IF WE ARE TO THINK RIGHTLY ABOUT AND (MORE IMPORTANT) PRAY TO THE HOLY SPIRIT.

The doctrine of the Trinity helps us see how all the clauses of the creeds are interrelated. The creeds are what we believe as Christians inspired by the Holy Spirit. That the Apostles' Creed is a baptismal creed is a reminder that belief in the Holy Spirit is not only confessed by the baptized, but it is also the Spirit into which Christians are baptized. The Spirit confirms what is confessed by those being baptized. Frequently, in the Acts of the Apostles (which some have said should have been called the Acts of the Holy Spirit), bold moves by the church in mission are usually prodded by and confirmed by the descent of the Holy Spirit.

The interrelation of the persons of the Trinity means that everything said about the Holy Spirit also ought to be said about the Father and the Son. Everything is related to everything in Christian theology, so repetition is not only inevitable but necessary. Christian belief is like an elegant web that is at once delicate but also strong. Leave out one part and the whole web collapses. Theology is the ongoing attempt to see the connections in the diverse narratives that make us Christian. A doctrine like the doctrine of the Trinity is a discovery that the church has made to keep us from leaving out any part of the story of God's care of creation through the calling into existence a people called *church*.

Will asked a distinguished church consultant, "Why do we have such uninteresting preaching and so many static, sedate congregations?" He expected the consultant to cite some organizational, institutional problem. Instead he was surprised to hear the consultant respond, "Neglect of the third person of the Trinity."

Come, Holy Spirit!

The Holy Spirit in Scripture

Though the doctrine of the Trinity is not explicitly named in scripture, we must start with scripture to understand why we even need a doctrine of the Trinity. That an elaborated "doctrine" of the Holy Spirit is not in scripture is not because the Holy Spirit is an unimportant character but because there are no "doctrines" or "dogmas" in scripture. Yet early on the church found it crucial to make explicit certain doctrines or dogmas to help us rightly read scripture.

Dogmas are, in the words of Robert Jenson, "irreversible rules of faith."[4] They set the boundaries for the arguments Christians must have to understand adequately what we believe. The dogmas of the church are often responses to the (mis)-interpretation of scripture, but they also are attempts to make sense of how Christians pray, worship, and live. For instance, we have a doctrine of the incarnation because we want to think boldly and carefully about the wonder of God being both fully human and fully divine in Jesus Christ. So to scripture we now turn, for it is there that we find why, after much controversy, Christians came to the judgment that the Holy Spirit must be understood as the third person of the Trinity.

We must begin with what Christians believe is our determinative creation story—the conception of Jesus in Mary's womb. The Holy Spirit initiated the Christian drama by impregnating a woman. Mary, who was engaged to Joseph, "became pregnant by the Holy Spirit" (Matt 1:18). In Luke the angel told Mary that "the Holy Spirit will come over you and the power of the Most High will overshadow you. Therefore, the one who is to be born will be holy. He will be called God's Son" (Luke 1:35). From the very beginning the Holy Spirit had a task. In the performance of that task *the Spirit did not call attention to herself because the Spirit's work is first and foremost to point to Jesus as the Son of the Father.* Just as the Spirit brooded over the waters at creation (Gen 1), so the fecund Spirit created at the beginning of the story is Jesus, God with us.

At the baptism of Jesus, the Spirit pointed to the meaning of Jesus; we can't figure out Jesus without the assistance of the

Holy Spirit. As Jesus came up from the water, the heavens were opened "to him, and he saw the Spirit of God coming down like a dove and resting on him" (Matt 3:16). Mark says, "While he was coming up out of the water, Jesus saw . . . the Spirit, like a dove, coming down on him" (Mark 1:10). Luke reports that not only did the Holy Spirit descend upon him, but John the Baptist said that whereas his baptism was of water, Jesus's baptism was of "the Holy Spirit and fire" (Luke 3:16).

These texts make clear the special relation between Jesus and the Spirit. Though it is unclear from the text, it seems that Jesus, and Jesus alone, saw the Holy Spirit at his baptism. This suggests a relation between Jesus and the Holy Spirit unlike any other, an intimacy between Jesus and the Holy Spirit that is rightly called *love*. Jesus and the Holy Spirit are united in common love of one another, and the Father loves Jesus and the Holy Spirit with that same love.

Accordingly these texts at the very beginning of the Gospels help us see the basic pattern that gives rise to the doctrine of the Trinity. The Father, Son, and Holy Spirit have distinct tasks, but they are united in performance of those tasks. Eugene Rogers puts it this way: "The Spirit proceeds from the Father to rest on the Son."[5] "What can the Spirit do that Christ cannot do better?" has found its answer. The Spirit rests on Jesus's body. The Spirit does so fully in unity with the Father and the Son. That *the Holy Spirit rests on Jesus's body* suggests to Rogers that the Spirit has a proclivity for the material, in particular, the materiality of the body. For those who believe that Christianity

13

is a vague, "spiritual" experience, the Holy Spirit's propensity to embodiment will be a challenge.

THE SPIRIT RESTS ON JESUS'S BODY.

So people come to the church saying, "I want to be more spiritual." The church responds, "Have some bread; take some wine." This is the response one might expect from a faith that sees the Holy Spirit as resting upon a body.

From early references in the Gospels to the Holy Spirit, we begin to see a pattern. Rogers says that just as Jesus's identity is established through the narrative of the Gospels, we know the character of the Spirit by observing how the Spirit interacts with plot and circumstance in the Gospels.[6] Rogers quotes Gregory of Nazianzus, the Eastern father whose work was decisive in showing the inseparability of Jesus and the Spirit. Gregory said: "Christ is born; the Spirit is His Forerunner. He is baptized; the Spirit bears witness. He is tempted; the Spirit leads Him up. He works miracles; the Spirit accompanies them. He ascends; the Spirit takes his place."[7]

This intimate relationship of Jesus and the Holy Spirit is nowhere more evident than when Jesus prayed. In Luke, after Jesus taught his disciples how to pray the Lord's Prayer, he told them that the heavenly Father would "give the Holy Spirit to those who ask him" (Luke 11:13). That gift to Jesus was evident as he prayed at the transfiguration (Luke 9:28-36) and even more powerfully shown as he prayed on the Mount of Olives (Luke 22:39-46). Though the Holy Spirit is not mentioned in these events, Christians have always read the Spirit present as Jesus prayed because through prayer Jesus was glorified by the Spirit.

In Romans 8:26-27 Paul says, "The Spirit comes to help our weakness. We don't know what we should pray, but the Spirit himself pleads our case with unexpressed groans. The one who searches hearts knows how the Spirit thinks, because he pleads for the saints, consistent with God's will." Rogers observes that this means that the fundamental prayer is the prayer that God alone can pray to God. Accordingly when we who are human pray to God, we "are caught up into the triune activity of the Persons praying one to another."[8] *Prayer makes possible our very participation in God's life, and the Holy Spirit makes prayer possible.*

Romans 8

"For all who are led by the Spirit of God are children of God. . . . When we cry, 'Abba! Father!' it is that very Spirit bearing witness with our spirit that we are children of God. . . . Likewise the Spirit helps us in our weakness; . . . that very Spirit intercedes with sighs too deep for words" (Rom 8:14-16, 26 NRSV).

As we noted, the temptation, particularly in the Western church, has been toward a binary account of God as Father and Son with the Spirit as afterthought. Christ can be made known, however, only through the Spirit. The intimate relation of Jesus and the Holy Spirit, indeed the intimacy between the

Father, Son, and Holy Spirit implied by scripture, has always been a challenge for the church to express. For example, the Christian East has always worried that the *filioque* clause in the Nicene Creed (the Holy Spirit proceeds from the Father *and the Son*) does not do justice to the relation of the Father and Holy Spirit. Eastern theologians, that is, Greek-speaking Christians, defend what they think of as the monarchy of the Father to emphasize that the Son and the Spirit equally have their source in the Father. The West, on the other hand, worries that the stress on the peculiar relationship between the persons of the Trinity characteristic of the Eastern church puts into question the unity of the divine persons.

Such disagreements must not distract us from the Nicene Council's agreement that *the work of each person of the Trinity is indivisible.* The Father is creator, and so are the Son and the Spirit. The Son is the redeemer, but then so are the Father and the Holy Spirit. In like manner the Spirit makes the Father and Son known to one another as well as to us, but the Father and the Son also make themselves known to one another and thus to us.

Relations between the persons of the Trinity are at the heart of Paul's hymn to the Spirit in Romans 8. Sarah Coakley has recently argued that in spite of the extraordinary theological achievement Nicaea represented, the creed tempts some to relegate the Spirit to the task of being merely the secondary communicator for the privileged dyad of Father and Son.[9]

Coakley calls attention to Romans 8:15-16, where Paul proclaims, "With this Spirit, we cry, 'Abba, Father.' The same

Spirit agrees with our spirit, that we are God's children." Coakley argues that in this passage the Spirit is given priority. When we pray we become part of a movement in which God answers God through our prayers.[10] The Spirit so identified is not based in our experience as individuals; prayer is not something done by oneself. *Prayer is a divine activity of God's call and response into which the one praying is drawn.*

Romans 8, therefore, is crucial if we are to understand how the Holy Spirit mediates Jesus to us. Indeed *mediation* may be too weak to describe the Spirit's work in humanity. In Romans 8:1-11 Paul tells us that through the Spirit we have become incorporated into the body of Christ. Thus Paul's strong claim that "if the Spirit of the one who raised Jesus from the dead lives in you, the one who raised Christ from the dead will give life to your human *bodies* also, through the Spirit that lives in you" (Rom 8:11, emphasis added).

BY THE HOLY SPIRIT'S DESCENT UPON THE BODY WE ARE MADE PARTICIPANTS IN THE LIFE OF THE TRINITY.

The Holy Spirit rests on the body of Jesus. In the next chapter we will explore why our belief in the "holy catholic and apostolic church" is appropriately included under our confession of the Holy Spirit as the third person of the Trinity. The church, as the body of Christ, implies that *by the Holy Spirit's descent upon the body we are made participants in the life of the Trinity.*

Integral to our confession of our belief in the Holy Spirit is our belief in the resurrection of the body. Because Christianity is an incarnational, bodily faith, we believe that there is nothing more spiritual than the body. The resurrection of Jesus was the resurrection *of a body*. While the Gospel accounts of Jesus's postresurrection appearances say that Christ's resurrected body moved through doors, was mistaken for a ghost or a gardener, appeared and disappeared, it is clear that the resurrection is an embodied event. In his resurrected body Christ continued in relationship with his disciples, ate and drank with them, showed up unexpectedly, and continued to take up room in the world. The presence of Christ among us, in the power of the Holy Spirit, is embodied. Few ideas are more detrimental to an understanding of the Holy Spirit, as presented in scripture or experienced in the church, than the notion that Christianity is essentially ethereal and spiritual rather than, by the descent of the Spirit, material and embodied. Jesus commanded us not only to love one another but to get down on our knees and wash someone's dusty feet (John 13:14). There's not much more carnal, somatic, and bodily than that.

The Advocate

That the Holy Spirit incorporates us into God's very life is not only found in the letters of Paul. In the Gospel of John, Jesus promised that though he would return to the Father, he would ask the Father to send the "Advocate," who would be with us forever. That "Advocate" is the "Spirit of truth" whom the disciples would recognize: "You know him, because he abides with you, and he will be in you" (John 14:16-17 NRSV). The advocate is sent to "teach you everything, and remind you of all I have said to you" (John 14:26 NRSV). The Spirit has distinct work to do: *to make us one body, the body of Christ.*

That the Holy Spirit is here called "Advocate" indicates that in Christ we are more than simply accepted by God or even justified by God. *The advocate continues to plead for us, to represent us to God in ways greater than our ways, and to speak on our behalf to God better than we could speak for ourselves.* At the same time *the advocate is God representing God to us, revealing God to us in ways that we could not have come up with on our own.*

That the Holy Spirit "will teach you everything, and remind you" of all that Jesus said is immensely reassuring. None of us is born Christian. We must learn the faith, and in the Holy Spirit we see that God loves us enough to teach us all we need to know to be with God. Jesus commands us to do some extraordinary things in his name but never commands us to attempt to obey him by ourselves. Jesus tells us some astounding truth that is easy to forget. Therefore the advocate reminds us. Here is truth we cannot teach ourselves, truth that is not only a great mystery to us but also truth that we, in our human sin, cannot attain on our own. Therefore the advocate is a truth-teller.

We know a person who suffered a great wrong at the hands of another. She was justifiably angry at the injustice perpetrated against her. In an encounter with her wrongdoer, our friend felt her rage boil over and she was in the process of giving him a piece of her mind. In that moment she "remembered that Christ commanded us to forgive our enemies. I said, 'Lord, I'll try to do what you want me to do, but you'll have to help me.'"

We believe her remembrance was the work of the advocate, the true eternal truth-teller, the teacher, the living reminder otherwise known as the Holy Spirit.

We spend most of our lives outside of the sacred precincts of the church. Thankfully, the advocate is with us forever, at all times and places, helping us to be the disciples Jesus calls us to be.

THE ADVOCATE, THE TRUE ETERNAL TRUTH-TELLER, THE TEACHER, THE LIVING REMINDER OTHERWISE KNOWN AS THE HOLY SPIRIT HAS DISTINCT WORK TO DO: *TO MAKE US ONE BODY, THE BODY OF CHRIST.*

Nicaea asserted the unwavering conviction that there has never been a time when God was not the Father, Son, and Holy Spirit. God coming to us as the Son or as the Holy Spirit is not a divine afterthought, a Plan B to which God was forced to resort after humanity messed up the Father's original intentions. Nor are the Son and the Holy Spirit only partially the truth about who God is. Jesus is the "full, perfect, and sufficient" revelation of God, as the church has historically taught.[11] When the Holy Spirit reveals God, there is no God waiting to offer more perfect revelation behind what the Holy Spirit reveals about God. To be sure, the birth, life, death, and resurrection of Jesus in human history are and were decisive for the recognition of God's triunity, but the fathers at Nicaea maintained that God has from eternity been triune. The Father did become the Father only when Jesus was conceived and born, but God has always been the Father, Son, and Holy Spirit before creation and before human time. God is the eternal Father, Son, and Holy Spirit; God determined from eternity to be for us and for us to be for God in the power of the Holy Spirit.

One way to say that the Trinity is eternal is by distinguishing between the *immanent* and the *economic* Trinity. The immanent Trinity is who God is, all the way down. The economic Trinity is the Trinity's actual work in history, the acts of God to which scripture gives witness, God in action. Catholic theologian Karl Rahner says that we must keep these two aspects of the Trinity, God's being and God's action, together. The immanent Trinity is the economic Trinity and the economic Trinity is the immanent Trinity. God is as God acts and God's action is God's being.[12]

Rahner stresses that some account of the immanent Trinity is needed to counter a heresy that many Christians assume without knowing it—*modalism*. Modalism is the belief that each person of the Trinity is but a different mode of God's being rather than a distinct person of God's being, that Father, Son, and Holy Spirit are merely diverse expressions or aspects of the one God. By maintaining that the persons of the Trinity eternally have an inner life, Rahner reminds us that God enjoys a communion with himself that is an expression of the mutual love between the persons of the Trinity. Relational, complete love is not just what God does but who God is.

God is the creator, redeemer, and sustainer, but creator, redeemer, and sustainer are not what it means to call God *Father*, *Son*, and *Holy Spirit*. When *creator*, *redeemer*, and *sustainer* are used to name the persons of the Trinity, it's usually a sign of modalism. We call God by the name Holy Spirit not because we have experienced some sort of spirit sustaining us. The Holy Spirit means more than our experience of the Holy Spirit. The Holy Spirit does more than "sustain" and the Holy Spirit has an identity that is more than the Holy Spirit's actions upon us. We call upon God as Holy Spirit because that's the proper name for God that we have been given by scripture.

One of the most influential accounts of the Trinity in recent times is John Zizioulas's depiction of *God as communion*. Zizioulas, an Orthodox theologian, says, "God is a relational being: without the concept of communion it would not be possible to speak of the being of God. . . . 'God' has . . . no true being apart from communion."[13] The Holy Spirit is not simply an impersonal force or a helpful aid in overcoming the distance between Christ and us; the Holy Spirit "is the person of the Trinity who actually realizes in history that which we call Christ, this absolutely relational entity, our Savior."[14] When God in Christ lovingly self-reveals to us, intervenes for us, tells the truth to us, judges us, or saves us and advocates for us before the throne of God, this is typical of the God who is essentially relational as Father, Son, and Holy Spirit.

We misunderstand the Holy Spirit if we do not always test our understandings by the affirmation that "in Christ God was" (2 Cor 5:19 NRSV). For example, when confronted by people who deny the existence of God, should we try to convince them that God exists? Usually, our arguments for God result in proving the existence of a god whom Christians don't worship, a deistic, nonrelational, nonloving, disembodied god who is less interesting than the Trinity. Deism usually begins with the world and works from the world toward the belief that there must be a god because "something had to start it all." After Deism's god got done with creation, god retired because the creator had nothing more to do. Such a "god" can never be as consequential and as relentlessly relational as the Trinity.

As modern people in the West, we have been taught to think of history as those events that humanity has produced in time. Now that Deism has rendered God inactive, it's up to us to make history come out right. There is no agency operative in history other than our own.

Christians believe the countercultural, peculiar claim that *through the Spirit God is active in history then and now*. History is to be found in the Bible, which, as the Fathers at Nicaea insisted, must be read in a trinitarian fashion. We believe, moreover, that the Spirit did not stop working after the first days of the church; the Spirit is present in all times and places, making Christ known, and in our baptism makes us participants in a story initiated and sustained by the Holy Spirit. How might our understanding of our time change if we spoke not of

American church history, but rather of the history of the Holy Spirit in America?

THE SPIRIT IS PRESENT IN ALL TIMES AND PLACES, MAKING CHRIST KNOWN, AND IN OUR BAPTISM MAKES US PARTICIPANTS IN A STORY INITIATED AND SUSTAINED BY THE HOLY SPIRIT.

To read the Bible in a trinitarian fashion means, for example, when we read that the "wind" swept over the waters at creation, that "wind" is the Holy Spirit at work even before we were given the name for the Holy Spirit. The same Spirit hovered over the waters of Mary's womb. The creative Spirit thus continues to make something where once there was nothing, continues to make a way when we thought there was no way. The work of the Holy Spirit is made explicit in the great thanksgiving prayer prayed over the waters for baptism as we make a new Christian. We pray:

Eternal Father:
When nothing existed but chaos,
    you swept across the dark waters
    and brought forth light.
In the days of Noah
    you saved those on the ark through water.
After the flood you set in the clouds a rainbow.
When you saw your people as slaves in Egypt,
    you led them to freedom through the sea.

Their children you brought through the Jordan
    to the land which you promised.
In the fullness of time you sent Jesus,
    nurtured in the water of a womb.
He was baptized by John and anointed by your Spirit.
He called his disciples
    to share in the baptism of his death and resurrection
    and to make disciples of all nations.
Pour out your Holy Spirit,
to bless this gift of water and *those* who *receive* it,
to wash away *their* sin
    and clothe *them* in righteousness
    throughout *their lives,*
that, dying and being raised with Christ,
    they may share in his final victory.[15]

As John Wesley once said, only a God who could create the world can create a Christian. This historic baptismal "flood prayer" reflects our conviction as Christians that *the God of the Old Testament is the same God who is found in Jesus Christ and the Holy Spirit.* We read three lessons from the Bible each Sunday; we believe that the Holy Spirit is present to help us locate ourselves in the ongoing story in the Old Testament of God's people. Accordingly the Spirit sanctifies the water of baptism, bringing saving life to that which otherwise could be quite deadly, just as Noah's family was saved on the ark. The Spirit blesses the bread of the Eucharist, enabling this to be for us the very presence of Christ, providing sacramental meeting.

THE HOLY SPIRIT IS PRESENT TO HELP US LOCATE OURSELVES IN THE ONGOING STORY IN THE OLD TESTAMENT OF GOD'S PEOPLE.

On Sunday, before scripture is read and proclaimed, we pray for the aid of the Holy Spirit, the advocate. No one can intelligently read, faithfully proclaim, clearly understand, and much less perform scripture alone. Fortunately, when it comes to hearing and obeying God's word, we are not left to our own devices. As Paul says, "The Holy Spirit comes to help our weakness" (Rom 8:26). In our struggles to bend our lives to the word, we have an advocate. Thus we pray before we read, "Open our hearts and minds by the power of your Holy Spirit, that, as the Scriptures are read and your Word proclaimed, we may hear with joy what you say to us today."[16]

Embodied Spirit

How fitting that a Holy Spirit, who rests upon Christ's body at his baptism and incorporates us into his church, forming us into the body of Christ, should often be best depicted in art. Though the Holy Spirit enables us to understand the word, the Holy Spirit is always more than words can say. One of the most compelling depictions of the Trinity is the famous icon by Andrei Rublev in which the three "men" visit Abraham and Sarah to tell them that in spite of their old age they would have a son (Gen 18:1-15). Rublev's icon depicts the three visitors sharing the meal Abraham had prepared. Though each one's face looks much like the others, each is dressed in different colors that Rublev thought appropriate to each person of the Trinity. In the original image, the Holy Spirit's clothing is blue, suggesting the Spirit's presence in sky and water.

Andrei Rublev, *Holy Trinity*, c. 1411, egg tempera on wood, State Tretyakov Gallery, Moscow. Courtesy Wikimedia Commons/DcoetzeeBot. The Holy Spirit is the figure on the right.

That Rublev positions the persons of the Trinity at a table on which the eucharistic elements are prominently displayed suggests the interconnection between our reading of scripture and our celebration of the liturgy. Central to the celebration of the Eucharist is the part of the eucharistic prayer known as the *Epiclesis*, in which the Holy Spirit is invoked:

We celebrate the memorial of our redemption, O Father, in
this sacrifice of praise and thanksgiving. Recalling his death,
resurrection, and ascension, we offer you these gifts.

Sanctify them by your Holy Spirit to be for your people
the Body and Blood of your Son, the holy food and drink of
new and unending life in him. Sanctify us also that we may
faithfully receive this holy Sacrament, and serve you in unity,
constancy, and peace; and at the last day bring us with all
your saints into the joy of your eternal kingdom.

All this we ask through your Son Jesus Christ: By him,
and with him, and in him, in the unity of the Holy Spirit all
honor and glory is yours, Almighty Father, now and for ever.
AMEN.[17]

This eucharistic prayer invoking the Spirit to sanctify the
body and blood of Christ and even to sanctify us is a dramatic
enactment of Paul's understanding of how the Holy Spirit
works. That work climaxes in Paul's rhetorical question, "Who
will separate us from Christ's love?" His answer: "I'm convinced
that nothing can separate us from God's love in Christ Jesus
our Lord: not death or life, not angels or rulers, not present
things or future things, not powers or height or depth, or any
other thing that is created" (Rom 8:38-39).

Paul's ringing confession that nothing can separate us from
the love of Christ is a testimony to the relational inner life of
the Trinity. Augustine, commenting on Paul's affirmation in
Romans 5:5 that God's love has been poured into our hearts
through the Holy Spirit, says this is so because God's love is the
relationship between the persons of the Trinity. While the persons of the Trinity are distinct, that doesn't mean they are three
gods; they are one in their common love of one another.[18] God

is the name of the love that constitutes the relation between the persons of the Trinity.

We must not spiritualize the love that determines the relation between the Father, Son, and Holy Spirit. By "spiritualize" we mean that process in which love is divorced from the Father's willingness to have the Son die on our behalf. As we noted earlier, the Holy Spirit rests on bodies and, in particular, on the body of the crucified Son who was tortured to death by a consortium of governmental and religious leaders egged on by the mob. Nothing is more excruciatingly corporeal than a crucified body.

In the Gospel of John, Jesus prays: "Righteous Father, even the world didn't know you, but I've known you, and these believers know that you sent me. I've made your name known to them and will continue to make it known so that your love for me will be in them, and I myself will be in them" (John 17:25-26).

The Holy Spirit points to Jesus on the cross and rests on Jesus on the cross. The love with which the Father and the Holy Spirit loved Jesus and the love with which Jesus loved the Father and the Holy Spirit is the love that refused to save Jesus from the cross. The love Jesus had for us led him to the cross. Augustine recommends, therefore, that we love Christ so that we might love one another. Such love is possible because what the scripture predicted has been fulfilled: "the Christ will suffer and rise from the dead on the third day" (Luke 24:46).

The love that is Trinity is a wonderful but also a harsh and dreadful love, love that suffers (as in Christ's crucifixion), love that (we learn in Christ's resurrection) cannot be destroyed. Christ's church is given the extraordinary opportunity to participate in the love that is God in a world that knows not God.

THE HOLY SPIRIT RESTS UPON BODIES, FIRST ON THE CRUCIFIED BODY OF JESUS, THEN ON THE OFTEN FULL-OF-HOLES AND BEATEN BODY OF CHRIST, THE CHURCH.

A little congregation in Alabama had been saving for a decade to build its own church and to move out of the rented space where it worshipped. A couple in the church had raised four foster children. One Sunday, during the prayers of intercession, the couple said that social services had asked them to take on three more children who had become homeless. They asked the church for prayers, "to help us find a larger place to rent so we can take in these kids."

With that, one of the oldest members of the congregation blurted out, "We don't need to pray for that. Let's give them our building fund money!" There was applause. That Sunday the church gave the entire building fund to enable the family to have a larger home. We believe that such a miracle is attributable only to having ordinary people pray, "Come, Holy Spirit!"

The Holy Spirit is the agent of the kingdom of God. That kingdom is present, often hidden, in the church. *The Holy Spirit is the way that God keeps actively loving us in time, the way that the Trinity keeps showing up to us, keeps pointing us toward the truth embodied in the crucified.* By God's love, we live in the age of the Spirit, that new time in which the church exists and testifies to the world that our time is not our own. God has taken time for us, and the sign of that divine intrusion is the Holy Spirit at work in the church that lives and works in the world.

God through the Spirit draws us into the life of the Trinity, making possible a people who would otherwise not exist. The Spirit must have a body on which the Spirit can rest. That body turns out to be called *church*. We are now ready, therefore, to explore the relation between the Holy Spirit and the church.

There are those who contrast the often-boring organizational, institutional church with the allegedly carefree, free-floating Holy Spirit. These tend to be the "I'm spiritual but not religious" crowd. Sorry. The Holy Spirit rests upon bodies, first on the crucified body of Jesus, then on the often full-of-holes and beaten body of Christ, the church.

Chapter Two

PENTECOST:
THE BIRTH OF THE CHURCH

When Pentecost Day arrived, they were all together in one place. Suddenly a sound from heaven like the howling of a fierce wind filled the entire house where they were sitting. They saw what seemed to be individual flames of fire alighting on each one of them. They were all filled with the Holy Spirit and began to speak in other languages as the Spirit enabled them to speak. (Acts 2:1-4)

A New People Created for a New Age

Pentecost. High drama—*at a church meeting!* They were gathered in one place, followers of Jesus who were wondering what his crucifixion meant for their relationship to this man. But then out of the heavens came the rush of a mighty wind, and tongues of fire came to rest on those present. Filled with the Holy Spirit, they began to speak in languages that were not their own. Under the power of the Holy Spirit, they spoke of God's deeds of power. Parthians, Medes, Elamites, and all the rest of the far-flung

Jewish diaspora, proselytes, Cretans, and Arabs heard in their own languages a new "thing" beginning. That new creation would bear the name *church*.

That the birth of the church by the Holy Spirit entailed the gift of languages is not accidental. At Babel humans had tried to reach to the heavens so that they might be as gods. The idea that they might be able to do so was made possible by the fact they spoke one language. That they spoke one language gave them the presumption that they were in control of their destiny. They entertained the prideful idea that they could cooperate in a manner so that everything was under their power, even a structure that would allow them to grab hold of the heavens.

In response to their attempt to be like God, they were punished by being separated from one another by different languages. Unable to communicate amid the babble, they became strangers to one another. At Babel the violence begun with Cain's fratricide of Abel (Gen 4) became the new normal in a world with no common language and many barriers to community. Humans were just enough like one another to fear the differences their diverse languages could not help but create.

Pentecost brought peace, not by healing differences through institutionalization of one language to replace the many. Instead a multilinguistic community was born to be for the world a witness to the peace instituted by the cross and resurrection of Jesus. Christians would be forced to learn the language of the stranger, Christ, because they also would be strangers to the world as a people of peace in a world of violence.

The Holy Spirit (always full of surprises) was particularly creative at Pentecost. Just as the wind had hovered over the waters at creation, just as the Spirit was present in Mary's womb, so now the Holy Spirit continued that initiating work by creating a people who "once were no people." As Nicholas Lash observes, the central metaphor for talk about God as Spirit is "breath." The Spirit breathed all creatures into being yet whispered gently to Elijah (1 Kgs 19:11-13), powerfully "strip[ped] the forests bare" (Ps 29:9), and still breathed peace on the disciples (John 20:22).[1] In short, the Spirit blows where it chooses (John 3:8), unsought, maybe even unwanted, intent on making all things new.

Who could have anticipated that a new people, Jew and Gentile, would be gathered to worship the God of Israel? How could such a miracle happen except as a gift of God, a gift akin to God's breathing life into mud to make humanity? The Holy Spirit has included even Gentiles in the promises of God to Israel. Paul tells the church at Ephesus, "You who were once so far away have been brought near by the blood of Christ. Christ is our peace. He made both Jews and Gentiles into one group. With his body, he broke down the barrier of hatred that divided us" (Eph 2:13-14). The Acts of the Apostles is the story of how, under the guidance of the Holy Spirit, the church was given the mission to be a showcase that the violence inherent in our babbling isolation from one another has been overwhelmed by the cross and resurrection of Christ.

THE ACTS OF THE APOSTLES IS THE STORY OF HOW, UNDER THE GUIDANCE OF THE HOLY SPIRIT, THE CHURCH WAS GIVEN THE MISSION TO BE A SHOWCASE THAT THE VIOLENCE INHERENT IN OUR BABBLING ISOLATION FROM ONE ANOTHER HAS BEEN OVERWHELMED BY THE CROSS AND RESURRECTION OF CHRIST.

Some who witnessed the gift of tongues at Pentecost thought that those who were possessed by the Spirit were drunk, under the influence, out of control. Peter, however, denied they were drunk, saying it's "only nine o'clock in the morning!" (Acts 2:15). (What would he have said if it had been five in the afternoon?) Then, under the power of the Spirit, Peter preached, drawing on the prophet Joel's dramatic apocalyptic imagery to indicate that a new age was beginning. His sermon would become the model for Christian preaching, proclaiming that Israel's long hopes were now fulfilled in the person of Jesus Christ. Remember where we left Peter in Luke's Gospel? Peter was unable to say one faithful word when confronted by the maid in the courtyard before Jesus's crucifixion (Luke 22:54-62). Now Peter boldly preached! No exclusively human explanation can account for Peter's homiletical courage. Peter's preaching is solid evidence for the reality of the Holy Spirit.

According to Peter the giving of the Spirit was nothing less than the advent of a new age inaugurated by the Holy Spirit. In former days, the Spirit was given to a few individuals, that is, prophets who had been empowered to speak God's truth. But there would come a day, prophesied Joel, when God's Spirit would be poured out upon all. That Spirit flood in the last days would result in prophetic sons and daughters, visionary young persons, and old folks daring to dream. Even slaves, men and women alike, would prophesy, all creation testifying that God is Lord of all. Now, *because of the descent of the Spirit, all, even those who were previously voiceless and hopeless, would be enabled to speak up and speak out in God's name.*

While a new age is inaugurated, bringing into existence a new people of that age, the essential mission of the Spirit remains the same: the Spirit continues to witness to Jesus by coming to rest on his body, thereby witnessing to a new age. Jesus, though seated at the right hand of the Father, was present in the power of the Holy Spirit poured upon all at Pentecost. The Spirit continues to rest on Jesus's body, only now that body turns out to be the church. The church, moreover, under the direction of the Spirit, has as its task—in word and deed—to point to Jesus. It is not accidental that the affirmation that we believe in the church is a clause that found its home in the third article of both the Apostles' and Nicene Creeds.

While Pentecost is appropriately celebrated as the birthday of the church, it's a mistake to think the work of the Spirit began at Pentecost. If we read the Old Testament as testimony to the Trinity, then we see the Spirit at creation, in the words of the prophets, in the gift of Torah, in leading God's people like a pillar of fire through whatever wilderness they wandered. Now that same Holy Spirit by which Jesus preached his first sermon in Nazareth (Luke 4) is poured out on ordinary people, young and old, high and low, to speak God's truth.

Thus Peter boldly proclaimed in his sermon that the work of the Spirit is no different from the work that Christ has done. To have the Spirit is not to have "more" than Christ, but rather *to have the Spirit is to have Christ*. The Holy Spirit does not enable us to say more than Christ, but it does enable us to speak of Christ, the one who has the power to forgive sins (Acts 2:37-39). Forgiveness in the power of the Holy Spirit makes possible a free people who do not have to live captive to the sins of the past. At the same time the Holy Spirit is truly the self-offering of Christ so that we need not await some more perfect, more complete truth of God. The Holy Spirit tells all (John 16:13).

THE SPIRIT CONTINUES TO REST ON JESUS'S BODY, ONLY NOW THAT BODY TURNS OUT TO BE THE CHURCH. THE CHURCH, MOREOVER, UNDER THE DIRECTION OF THE SPIRIT, HAS AS ITS TASK— IN WORD AND DEED—TO POINT TO JESUS.

A close relation between Christ and the Spirit is exactly what we should expect if God is Trinity. As we said earlier, *God* indicates the indissoluble relation of the Father, Son, and Holy Spirit. Claude Welch puts the matter just right in saying, "One cannot possibly speak of the dependence of the church on Jesus Christ without at the same time understanding that our participation in him is in and through the Spirit and that our common life is a sharing in his relation to the Father, in the household of God."² We cannot, in our sin and lies, come to God, so God in Jesus Christ comes to us, takes hold, draws us near, forgives us, relates to us even as Father, Son, and Holy Spirit relate in love. The church, as the very body of Christ, is a visible sign of the intimacy that God intends for all through the redemptive, relational power of the Holy Spirit.

Christ's redeeming and reconciling work remains his, but that same redeeming and reconciling work is imparted by the Spirit to the church. "Thus the Holy Spirit makes alive, reveals Christ to us and enables us to say Jesus is Lord, seals us in Christ, gives new birth to enter the kingdom, enables us to call God Father and pours his love into our hearts."³ *Through the Spirit the church becomes for the world Christ's body, the way the world is given continuing, bodily assurance that Jesus Christ is Lord.*

Jane showed up at Marjorie's door early one morning.⁴ Marjorie was in the last stages of a terminal illness. "The church asked me to stop by and pray with you," explained Jane. After a few minutes of conversation, Marjorie tearfully revealed that she had prayed to God for support and reassurance but said, "I feel alone, as if God has forgotten me."

"Marjorie," Jane responded, "I want you to believe that God sent me. Maybe I'm the way God showed up and answered your prayers."

Jane's comment catches some of the power of service to a Holy Spirit who settles upon and empowers witness, even in the church.

Divine and Human

That the Spirit unites Christ with his church is analogous to the movement of God to Christ in which the Spirit fully unites Christ's humanity with Christ's divinity. The church is the body of Christ just as Jesus is fully human as the incarnate deity. Though perhaps a bit misleading, it can be said that the humanity and divinity of the incarnation is analogous to the relation of the body of Christ to the church. Some develop this analogy by suggesting the identification of Christ with the church through the Spirit means the church is an extension of the incarnation. ("The church is Christ's presence in the world"; "Our hands are the hands of Christ, doing his work"; and other preacherly exaggerations.) As tempting as such a description may be, for the church to be so described risks losing the truth that only in Jesus was God fully incarnate. We are not the presence in the world of an otherwise absent Christ. Christ is at work in the world, drawing all things unto himself—in the power of the Holy Spirit—whether or not we work with him. *The church, by the aid of the Holy Spirit, is the witness to the one who alone is incarnate, but the church is not the incarnation.* The church is the witness to the incarnation by the gift of the Spirit.[5] But the church is of the Holy Spirit through gift, not by nature.

The interdependence of Christology and ecclesiology can be illustrated by how christological mistakes (otherwise known as *heresies*) distort how one thinks about the church. Stephen Pickard suggests that the classical christological heresies of Docetism and Ebionism have implications for how the church is understood. *Docetism* was the view held by those who believed Christ could not be fully human if he were fully divine. For Docetists, Christ only *appeared* to be human (Greek, *dokein*, "to appear"), but because he was God he could not fully share our humanity. For Christ fully to share our humanity would be a diminishment of God's divinity. Ebionites, in contrast to Docetists, regarded Jesus as fully human and therefore they denied that he could be fully divine.[6]

Pickard says *Docetism often entails an inflated understanding of the significance of the church.* A Docetic understanding of the church emphasizes the church's divine nature in a manner that ignores the church's humanity. Docetists have the problem of then explaining why the church is so often compromised and corrupted. They try to explain how the church can be God's very body yet corrupt by distinguishing between the "visible" and "invisible" church. The divine nature of the church is identified with the invisible church. Just as Jesus only appeared to be human, a spirit inhabiting a human body, Docetists think the *real* church is invisible, spotless, and pure, a divine event trapped in an often grubby human institution.

Pickard notes Karl Barth's argument that a Docetic understanding of the church cannot help but transform the Christian faith into a form of *Gnosticism*. Gnosticism (Greek, *gnōsis*, "knowledge") is that heresy that makes the Christian faith into arcane, secret knowledge held by an enlightened few. Christianity is presented as a set of disembodied ideas, a philosophy of the divine that denies the earthly reality whom Christians worship—a crucified Jew. Gnostics tend to believe the empirical church, Saint John's down the street, cannot be the "real" church. The real church is an invisible fellowship of the Spirit, something of the heart removed from the often-sordid church here and now.[7]

A Docetic understanding of the church as free from sin often sees the world as unredeemable. The church must work to keep itself unspotted by a fallen world. Pickard suggests that *Manicheanism*, the heresy that maintained that materiality is evil, is the natural ally of a Docetic view of the church, in which an idealized church is contrasted to a lost world in a manner that results in a detached, spiritualized, romantic characterization of what it means to be a Christian in the world.

Pickard also thinks that a Docetic ecclesiology results in a church that craves secular political power. After Constantine's establishment of Christianity as the religion of the Roman Empire, a church grown prideful modeled itself on forms of hierarchical authority that betrayed the communal character of the church.[8] Christian ethics became the worldly-wise power of the church. This made it impossible for Christians to live as disciples of Christ. In particular, the nonviolent character of Jesus's teaching was lost.

In contrast to Docetic understandings of the church, an Ebionite ecclesiology presumes the church is but another human institution, subject to the same sociological limitations and characteristics of all merely human institutions. Ebionites assume that the church should be a helpful social institution, an organization that "meets the needs of people." The church at its best, for the Ebionite, is much like any other caring institution in society except that the church cares more. The problem with such a view is not only does the church become whatever consumers want it to be, but we lose any sense that the church is not our creation. The church is not simply a means whereby humans get what we want out of God but is God's appointed means of getting what God wants from us. The church is the product of and accountable to the Holy Spirit.

In his sermon in Acts 2, Peter claims that we are in the last days because the Spirit has given a fresh dispensation due to the resurrection of Jesus. Peter's imagery is stirring and apocalyptic; the beginning of a new age is not an everyday affair. The church is the embodiment of redemption; there is now, by God's grace, an alternative to the world. That's why it is so important not to dismiss the church as just another human creation.

THE MYSTERY OF THE CHURCH IS THAT IT IS, BY GOD'S GOOD GRACE, MORE THAN IT SEEMS TO BE. THE HOLY SPIRIT IS THE "MORE" OF THE CHURCH.

Just as Pickard says that a correlative of a Docetic ecclesiology was a Manichean view of the world, so he thinks an Ebionite ecclesiology underwrites a Pelagian understanding of the human condition. *Pelagianism* was that heresy that is alleged to have maintained that we could effect our own salvation. Augustine opposed both Manicheanism and Pelagianism. He recognized that like Docetism and Ebionism, the Manicheans and Pelagians were mirror images of one another. Each of these heresies in its own way refused to accept the mystery of the incarnation as well as the wonder of the church. *The mystery of the church is that it is, by God's good grace, more than it seems to be.* The Holy Spirit is the "more" of the church.

Pickard shows how christological heresies have ecclesial expression in the church in Europe and North America, which he characterizes as caught between being "fast-asleep churches" or "frenetic churches."[9]

The fast-asleep church is the self-satisfied church that boringly recycles habits and ways of the past without attending to changing social circumstances or to the machinations of the Holy Spirit. Fast-asleep churches are comatose, but their Docetic presumptions keep these churches from acknowledging their demise or knowing what to do about it. They are unable to recognize their loss of purpose partly because they have grown lazy having for so long inhabited a culture that they assumed was Christian. That assumption blinded them to the distinctive calling the Holy Spirit gives the church.[10] Ignoring the sad state of their institution, they continue to assert that the church is a spiritual entity that shouldn't be judged by human standards.

The frenetic church frantically enacts programs to arrest decline and restore the church's lost social status, perhaps even making the church once again politically powerful. Churches that Pickard identifies as frenetic embody the Ebionite alternative because they believe it is up to them to make the church the church through savvy application of the latest sociological, institutional, or leadership insights. Curiously, such an understanding of the church results in accommodation to the prevailing culture in a way not unlike that of the fast-asleep church.

Both ways of understanding the church fail to trust the Holy Spirit as the agent of renewal. Such trust is at the heart of our confession that we believe in the "holy catholic and apostolic church." We believe in the church because we trust the "Holy Spirit, the Lord, the giver of life." The church exists only because the fecund Holy Spirit animates our lives, bringing into existence the church. Much of the time as Christians we confess belief in things we can't see; here we confess belief in the visible church, warts and all, as an act of faith that the church is a gift of God in the power of the Holy Spirit. We hesitate to so describe our faith in the church because such a description might suggest that, given the church's failure to be true to the task God has given us, faith may simply be a way of expressing an irrational commitment to believing that, all evidence to the contrary, the church matters.

That is not why we say we believe in the church. We confess belief in the church because *we believe that the church would not exist if God in the person of the Holy Spirit did not call the church into existence.* As we have tried to show by developing the connections between our christological convictions and our understanding of the church, we do not believe in the church itself; only God is "believed in." But we do believe the church because we believe that there God has condescended to be present in word and sacrament, though present in a manner different from, for instance, our presence to one another.

That's why Rowan Williams suggests that the creeds do not invite us to believe *in* the church but rather *our creeds ask us to believe the church.*[11] By the power of the Holy Spirit, we believe that the church's witness to the faith is true, that despite its faults (which are many) the church is the primary way God has chosen to be God with us. A disembodied spirit is not the Holy Spirit. The church is not our creation, but rather through the Holy Spirit the church is God's new creation, birthed by the Spirit at Pentecost, God's gift for the world's salvation.

Lives Out of Control

The Holy Spirit is the breath of God; that breath and wind are central images the Bible uses to describe the Holy Spirit suggest that *the Holy Spirit is a wild, unpredictable character.* Nicholas Lash puts it this way: "To confess God as Spirit is to acknowledge that the world is not under our control, nor is that of any other creature, system, force, or thing, for everything is breathed by God. To pledge ourselves pliable to God the Spirit may breed anarchy but it undoubtedly sets our face against all forms of fatalism."[12] Life in the Spirit, Christian discipleship, is rightly construed as life out of our control because we live by borrowed breath. We in the modern world enjoy thinking that we have at last come to the point in human development when we live under no control other than self-control. At Pentecost we discovered that the lives we are living are not our own. Because the Holy Spirit not only enters our time but also commandeers our lives, we can hope for lives that are adventuresome—even wild and unpredictable.

What happened at Pentecost could not have been anticipated any more than creation itself could have been anticipated. The Holy Spirit is the life-giving power that is able to create and then to sanctify and to grow a new community. Through the Spirit a variety of gifts constitute the life of the church (1 Cor 12). Life in this community is marked by the *fruit of the Spirit*: "love, joy, peace, patience, kindness, goodness, faithfulness, gentleness, and self-control" (Gal 5:22-23). With the Spirit comes freedom from the bondage to sin and death (Rom 8:2), making possible lives of love because love is the first fruit of the Spirit.[13] For those of us who live in the modern, Western world, the Spirit brings freedom from bondage to ourselves, freeing us for love of others and from that widespread contemporary perversion of our humanity—narcissism.

The work of *the Holy Spirit can take a variety of forms that reflect the particular cultural and historical institutions and habits in which the church finds itself.* As we have noted, it is of the nature of the Holy Spirit to rest upon the body of Christ, therefore to descend to us where we are and to communicate God to us in ways we can comprehend, healing the chaos and confusion of Babel. That doesn't mean that Christian worship is arbitrary, but that Christians must always be ready to be enriched by the diverse ways in which the Trinity makes itself known to us in the power of the Holy Spirit, leading us places we would not venture on our own.

THE WORK OF THE HOLY SPIRIT CAN TAKE A VARIETY OF FORMS THAT REFLECT THE PARTICULAR CULTURAL AND HISTORICAL INSTITUTIONS AND HABITS IN WHICH THE CHURCH FINDS ITSELF.

The church has always had a challenge in keeping up with the living, free, and (to our limited minds) sometimes disruptive Holy Spirit. For instance, some churches believe that those who bear the responsibility to be pastors should, like Matthias, be chosen by lot (Acts 1:12-26). Many think that is an irresponsible way to identify clergy. But it's an interesting question. What kind of church would we need to be to call people to leadership who are chosen by lot? We would need to be a church in which every member bears real responsibilities and could be called to lead at any time. Churches that defend careful (often laborious) vetting of new clergy and rigid, hierarchical views of ministry ought to admit that we are a long way from the seemingly flexible, ad hoc, Spirit-initiated leadership depicted in the Acts of the Apostles. Even in churches in which ministerial leadership is not chosen by lot, in actual practice the way people become clergy in many of our churches is close to a form of casting lots! *The Holy Spirit, thank God, has not left the church to its own merely human devices.*

The church is never free to make decisions about its life together on the basis of "what works for us." Word, sacrament, and ministry have been regarded by most Christians through the centuries as necessary for the church to be the church. These practices are the concrete and visible means "through which Christ gives himself to be present to his church, as determinative patterns of common life which through the power of the Spirit are lifted up to be instruments for the realization and sustenance of new life in Christ."[14]

What is crucial for the authenticity of word, sacraments, and ministry is how they must avoid calling attention to themselves given that their *faithfulness requires submission to the Holy Spirit task of always pointing to Jesus.* That's one reason why the best sermons are transparent, sermons that point to Christ and away from the person of the preacher or the alleged fidelity of the congregation. The most faithful Christian leaders are those who serve Christ and his people rather than themselves. It's not so much that the bread on the altar is holy because it is consecrated by the priest in the proper liturgical manner, but rather that the bread is holy in that being blessed for God's people it points them toward Christ.

James Kay characterizes preaching as a human work but one undertaken in concert with the Holy Spirit:

> Preaching can only be undertaken as prayer. Our words do not control or constitute the new creation. They are witnesses to the living God, but they are not God. . . . All sermon preparation therefore must be a prayer for the Holy Spirit to take our ordinary words, however eloquent or inarticulate, and make them the bread of life. Here the sermon,

on analogy with the Lord's Supper, is always a matter of *epiclesis* or invocation. . . . [However] sermons should call forth the preacher's best efforts . . . we cannot appeal to divine agency as excluding or denigrating human agency, even as we confess boldly that "we have this treasure in clay jars, so that it may be made clear that this extraordinary power belongs to God and does not come from us" (2 Corinthians 4:7). Come Creator Spirit![15]

The Holy Spirit and the Mission of the Church

Through word, sacrament, and ministry the Spirit makes us witnesses to Jesus Christ. The gospel requires witnesses because Jesus is not some general truth that can be known without an ongoing community of people who have witnessed specifically to him across space and time. The truth toward which we witness is not some vague generality like love, peace, or justice; this truth is a person on whom the Holy Spirit rests, Jesus Christ. Acts is the record of the beginning of the work of the Holy Spirit's calling into existence a people who must exist in physical, bodily form to make known what God has done in Christ in human history. The Holy Spirit is "storied" in Acts as we are given the eyes to see, through Luke's narrative, the church rejected and persecuted, cast down by the powers that be, and then raised up and driven forward by the Spirit as an encroachment of God's kingdom.

In his book on Acts, *World Upside Down: Reading Acts in the Graeco-Roman Age,* our colleague Kavin Rowe notes that you don't have to wait long in Acts before being introduced to Luke's programmatic thesis: after they have received "the power of the Holy Spirit," the risen Jesus tells them they "shall be my witnesses in Jerusalem and in all Judea and Samaria to the end of the earth" (Acts 1:8).[16] Such a mission is required because the disciples were to make known to the world that Jesus, not Caesar, was Lord. That claim was not an attempt by Christians to grab power and to take over the role of Caesar; they proclaimed that Jesus's lordship was more radical than Caesar imagined. The witness of the disciples entailed a politics that was more threatening than Rome and all other worldly powers could comprehend. It is therefore not surprising that the disciples found themselves constantly in trouble. Why was the church so disruptive and so threatening to controlling politicians? Blame it on the out-of-control Holy Spirit.

In the fifth chapter of Acts we are told that the apostles were arrested and put in prison. During the night the angel of the Lord opened the prison doors. Rather than hightailing it out of town, the apostles went right to the temple publicly to "tell the people everything" about the life of Jesus (Acts 5:20). Brought before the council, they were ordered not to teach in the name of Jesus. Peter and the apostles refused that compromise because they "must obey God rather than humans!" (Acts 5:29). They then proclaimed everywhere that though those who would have them silenced had killed Jesus by hanging him on a tree, God had raised up Jesus that Israel might repent. The disciples confessed that they only knew this to be true because

51

they "are witnesses of such things, as is the Holy Spirit, whom God has given to those who obey him" (Acts 5:32).

Acts shows that the Spirit's work was a shock to some of the apostles whom the Spirit led to bring the word even to those who were not Israel. Summoned by Roman army officer Cornelius, one of Caesar's finest, Peter preached to Cornelius's household even though they were Gentiles. He did so because he had a dream that he at first thought questioned whether Jewish dietary practices were applicable to Gentile converts. Then in bringing the word even to a Gentile army officer like Cornelius, Peter discovered that the dream was about "unclean" people. Peter preached about Jesus's baptism, his anointing by the Holy Spirit, and his crucifixion and resurrection. Peter knew all this was true because he and the *apostles had been chosen by God to be witnesses, witnesses who were unable to contain or to control the Holy Spirit as it leapt over one boundary after another*, most dramatically moving even to Gentiles like Cornelius.

While Peter was still speaking, the Holy Spirit fell on all his listeners, who began, as those at Pentecost had done, to speak in tongues. Challenged by some who thought one could only be baptized if circumcised as a Jew, Peter asked rhetorically: "These people have received the Holy Spirit just as we have. Surely no one can stop them from being baptized with water, can they?" (Acts 10:47). The word was proclaimed under the compulsion of the Holy Spirit and the word was received by the action of the Holy Spirit. The unexpected reach of God to Gentile outsiders was thus confirmed by the Holy Spirit. That pattern—the word proclaimed and received as Jesus—across the centuries has determined the authenticity of the ministry of the word.

In Acts Paul is the paradigmatic Holy Spirit agent who exemplifies how the word explodes throughout the world. Often imprisoned, even more often rejected, Paul, with the aid of the Holy Spirit, founded and nourished churches across the Roman Empire. Particularly interesting is Paul's encounter at Ephesus with some "disciples" who seemed to count themselves followers of Jesus. Paul asked them if they had received the Holy Spirit when they were baptized. They responded that not only had they not received the Holy Spirit, they had never even heard of the Holy Spirit. It seems they had been baptized into the earlier baptism associated with John the Baptist. In effect they had not been baptized. In the only instance of rebaptism in the New Testament, Paul baptized them "in the name of the Lord Jesus," and when he laid his hands on them, they received the Holy Spirit, spoke in tongues, and prophesied (Acts 19:1-7). Note that *baptism "in the name of the Lord Jesus" is inextricably baptism in the Holy Spirit—the Holy Spirit is not optional equipment for Christians.* Witness, discipleship, lives out of our control and under the control of God are the fruit of the Spirit.

BAPTISM "IN THE NAME OF THE LORD JESUS" IS INEXTRICABLY BAPTISM IN THE HOLY SPIRIT— THE HOLY SPIRIT IS NOT OPTIONAL EQUIPMENT FOR CHRISTIANS.

The Holy Spirit seems to have induced wild diversity in the early church. That some followers of John the Baptist thought of themselves as Christians is an indication that early Christians were all over the map as they sought to discover what it meant to be a follower of Jesus. That process is not over because we serve a living God; under the guidance of the Spirit Christians can expect to be shocked by gospel implications they had not anticipated. That's the effect the Holy Spirit has upon the body of Christ in motion.

So when we pray, "Come, Holy Spirit!" it's as if we pray, "Bring it on, Holy Spirit! Shake us up, send us forth, kick us out, and make us a more interesting church than we would be if you had left us alone!"

The Holy Spirit as Disruptor, Teacher, Guide, and Judge of the Church

The early church, under the guidance of the Holy Spirit, slowly came to some consensus about what really mattered. Christians decided that what counted was scripture. They also came to a consensus about what authority scripture had and which rites were necessary for the church's existence. The church came to a consensus about the role of its leaders. Of course each of these developments, significant as it certainly was, only produced further controversy. That Christians had disagreements is a sign that for the church truth matters and what counts as truth is often discovered through controversy. Few of us enjoy conflict, but *sometimes our controversy demon-*

strates that the Holy Spirit is continuing to energize and to reveal truth to the church.

It is the nature of the Holy Spirit to shake up the church, particularly when the church becomes self-satisfied and content with the status quo. For instance, there is still disagreement between churches on whether there are two sacraments—baptism and Eucharist—or seven. Perhaps that argument (between Catholics and Protestants) ought better be framed not by arguing about the number of sacraments but rather by agreement on the purpose of our sacramental worship. We like the way that Claude Welch speaks of the interplay between Spirit and word, sacrament, and ministry:

> Word, sacrament and ministry together are structures of human existence taken up by the Spirit (which is to say, given to the church) and used as means whereby the grace of Christ is given, the power of new life made effectual, communicated through the historical life of the people of God. At the same time they are signs and instruments of the promise that Christ is even now newly presenting himself to his people and taking them into his new humanity.[17]

The special relationship of the Spirit and the church doesn't mean that the work of the Holy Spirit is limited to the church. The Spirit that gave life at creation, that breathed life into Adam, is the same Spirit that came on those gathered at Pentecost. The same Spirit who breathed new life into the dry bones of Israel (Ezek 37:1-14) is the same Spirit at work in the world, gathering into the church those who once knew not the name of Jesus. The same Spirit that drove the fledgling church in Acts toward even the Gentiles is the Spirit that today makes settled, introverted congregations uneasy with the way they have limited the work of the Spirit to the care, internal maintenance, and safekeeping of the church.

THE SPECIAL RELATIONSHIP OF THE SPIRIT AND THE CHURCH DOESN'T MEAN THAT THE WORK OF THE HOLY SPIRIT IS LIMITED TO THE CHURCH.

Rowan Williams notes the Spirit's work outside the church by saying that the church is "meant to be the place where Jesus is active in the world. And once we have said that, we can turn it around and say that where Jesus is visibly active, something like the church must be going on."[18] This doesn't mean that the visible church, its teaching and sacraments, don't matter; it is simply to recognize that at times we learn what is most important for the church by looking beyond its visible boundaries. Though the Holy Spirit birthed the church, the Holy Spirit intends to have more of the world than the church.

Williams says that if we look at the current state of the church from the viewpoint of the Spirit, we must ask some "awkward questions" about how we have let ourselves be distracted so that the Bible and sacraments, as well as the Christ whose life is the heart of the church, are not at the center of church life. It is important to trust the Holy Spirit to work even in those churches that are in decline as well as those churches that seem to flourish. The Spirit has always challenged the church from unexpected directions. It is, therefore, not without reason that we pray to the Spirit, "Do it again!" so that our church might recover a radical sense of what God wants us to be.[19]

At this point you may be thinking that our account of the Holy Spirit's birth and care of the church has little to do with the church you attend. The current church, at least the white, middle-class, mainstream Protestant church, seems sick. *Where has the Spirit gone?* Maybe the Spirit is where she always is, making Jesus known but in ways that are judgment on the church.

The person who claims to receive more inspiration from a Broadway play, or who says he or she feels a greater spirit of loving community at a rock concert than at church, speaks judgment upon a church devoid of Spirit. It is therefore not by accident that in the Nicene Creed, immediately following our confession that we believe in "the one holy catholic and apostolic church," there is the acknowledgment of "one baptism for the forgiveness of sins." Because the church is a human institution, God has given it all it needs (forgiveness) to be holy. As Welch says, "The being of the church is not something apart from the fellowship, it is the community of [sinners] in which Christ exercises his Lordship."[20]

An essential mark of the church is catholicity. The church catholic is a church in union with God and one another. Unity, at least the unity that comes with the Holy Spirit, is not oppressive uniformity. *The fellowship in the Spirit makes Christians love one another and, in particular, love one another for how our differences are crucial for the upbuilding of the body of Christ. In*

1 Corinthians 12, Paul calls the Corinthians to attend to the variety of gifts that make up the body of Christ. "A demonstration of the Spirit is given to each person for the common good" (1 Cor 12:7). For Paul, whether or not a spiritual gift is of the *Holy* Spirit is whether or not that gift edifies the church. People today often speak of the Spirit as individual and personal when, as we have seen, the Holy Spirit is intensely communal and corporate.

The catholicity of the church, that Christians are in fundamental unity with Christ and one another through baptism, makes our disunity sad. We in the church ought to confess the sin of our divisions, admitting that our most tragic divisions are not between Catholic and Protestant or Protestant denominations but the divisions between rich and poor, Caucasians and people of color, the disabled and those who are "healthy," the young and the old. The church ought to be a showcase for what the Holy Spirit can do. It is to our shame that Christians willingly kill one another in the name of national loyalties or love our religion by hating other faiths. Is it any wonder that non-Christians find our disunity a confirmation that we do not believe what we say we believe?

That we are citizens of a kingdom made possible by the forgiveness of our sins gives us hope for reconciliation with one another. That is what we confess when we say we believe in "one holy catholic church." Most of us live lives of far too much compromise to think of ourselves as holy. But holiness is first and foremost an attribute of the whole church, not a characteristic of pious individuals. To affirm that the church is holy is not a denial of our sin but rather an affirmation of the power of the Spirit to overwhelm our isolation from one another through the creation of this new community capable of recognizing and confessing that we as the church have often betrayed our calling. The holy church is the one church.

Jesus prayed for the church that "they will be one" (John 17:21). In a world of boundaries, tensions, old wounds, and separations in the body of Christ, the church has little hope of ever being holy, catholic, and *one* except by praying, "Come, Holy Spirit!"

Chapter Three

HOLINESS: LIFE IN THE SPIRIT

John and Charles Wesley sought to renew the Church of England by having Christians take seriously that they were called to live holy lives. The Wesleys stressed that every Christian should be sanctified. *Sanctification* is the term used to describe the work of the Holy Spirit to free our lives from sin. Accordingly John and Charles sought to discover modes of life—holiness—that would aid Christians in their desire to be freed from sin and on the way to salvation.

Because John and Charles Wesley were so earnest and organized in their desire for holiness, they often were subject to derision and ridicule. At Oxford those who gathered around John Wesley were given the nickname *Holy Club*. *Methodist* was originally a name meant to ridicule Wesley for being too "methodical" in his understanding of how Christians should live. Methodists were labeled by many in the Church of England as "enthusiasts." That was not a compliment; an enthusiast was thought to have a dangerously emotional, nonintellectual understanding of the faith.

SANCTIFICATION IS THE TERM USED TO DESCRIBE THE WORK OF THE HOLY SPIRIT TO FREE OUR LIVES FROM SIN.

Yet John and Charles Wesley were convinced that holiness was what it meant to be a Christian. Influenced by Eastern Christian theologians, John Wesley appropriated their accounts of "divinization" into his idea of "perfection." There is no stronger expression of this emphasis on holiness than Charles Wesley's hymn "Love Divine, All Loves Excelling":

Finish, then, thy new creation;
pure and spotless let us be.
Let us see thy great salvation
perfectly restored in thee;
changed from glory into glory,
till in heaven we take our place,
till we cast our crowns before thee,
lost in wonder, love, and praise.[1]

We are so familiar with "Love Divine, All Loves Excelling" that the extraordinary claims of this hymn can be missed. Was Charles Wesley serious when he asked God to make us "pure and spotless"? He was quite serious. Like his brother, John, Charles desired for himself and for all Christians that as far as possible we lead lives free of sin. *Each of us should want to be the "humble dwelling" in which the Spirit makes a home.* Accordingly Charles Wesley hoped that we might in this life "serve thee as thy hosts above," which implies that the communion the saints enjoy in heaven is possible here on earth below.

One of the words John Wesley used to describe the holiness characteristic of the Christian life was *perfection*. He did not think that Christians could be free of ignorance or mistakes, but he did think that through the work of Christ made present by the Holy Spirit, Christians could be freed from "outward sins." According to Wesley, "the fullness of time is now come, the Holy Ghost is now given, the great salvation of God is brought unto men by the revelation of Jesus Christ. The kingdom of heaven is now set up on earth."[2]

Note the last line of Charles Wesley's hymn—"Lost in wonder, love, and praise." To be sanctified is not to try very hard to achieve some impossible ideal. That misconception of holiness can lead to narcissistic self-righteousness or to perpetual guilt. "To be made perfect" from a Wesleyan perspective is to be caught up so completely in the life of the Holy Spirit you are not burdened by constant self-doubt. *To be sanctified is to be drawn into a way of life so compelling that our worry that we may not be doing enough for God is lost.* The saints never try to be saints; it just turns out that way as a gift of the Holy Spirit.

That many people doubt perfection is possible Wesley attributed to mistaken ideas about the Holy Spirit's perfecting work. Wesley argued that in scripture perfection is "pure love reigning alone in our heart and life."[3] Perfection so understood means our hearts are so filled with love that all our words and actions are accordingly governed. Yet Wesley warned that simply to "feel" we are free from sin is inadequate. We should never believe that the work of love is finished "till there is added the testimony of the Spirit, witnessing his entire sanctification as clearly as his justification."[4]

Wesley understood justification and sanctification to be intertwined; you could not have one without the other. For Wesley *justification* names what Christ has done for us in gaining pardon from God for our sins. Yet at the very moment of justification, sanctification begins. According to Wesley, real change is worked in us by the Holy Spirit:

> We are inwardly renewed by the power of God. We feel "the love of God shed abroad in our heart by the Holy Ghost which is given unto us" [*cf.* Rom. 5:5], producing love to all mankind, and more especially to the children of God, expelling the love of the world, the love of pleasure, of ease, of honour, of money, together with pride, anger, self-will and every other evil temper; in a word, changing the "earthly, sensual, devilish mind" into "the mind which was in Christ Jesus" [*cf.* Phil. 2:5].[5]

Wesley's extravagant sanctificationist claims may sound as if he has a too-sanguine view of human nature. Is it realistic of Wesley to claim that our spirits are so sweepingly transformed that all "love of the world" is expelled from us?

John Wesley had a robust, orthodox view of human depravity and sinfulness. But he had an even more exuberant assessment of the power of the Holy Spirit to transform lives warped by sin. *Grace* for Wesley meant not some saccharine view of human nature (God says, "I love you just the way you are; promise me you won't change a thing"). Wesleyan *grace is the power of the Holy Spirit working in us to give us lives we could not have had without the Spirit's work.*

Wesleyan sanctification is a "gradual process" that begins as soon as we are "born again." As Jesus told Nicodemus, the "Spirit blows wherever it wishes" (John 3:8), making us as if we were newborn, dead to sin and alive to God. We should, therefore, desire "entire sanctification"; that is, we should want freedom from pride, self-will, anger, and unbelief. We should want to "go on toward perfection" (Heb 6:1 NRSV) so that love takes over our lives, excluding the hold sin has over us. To be sanctified is to have a kind of "spiritual light" in the soul supplying an evidence of "things unseen."[6] Faith, for Wesley, was the assurance that by the power of the Holy Spirit, the same dynamic of cross and resurrection that characterized the life, death, and resurrection of Jesus characterizes us.

Something from Another World

We began this chapter with the observation that Methodism was a holiness movement. Note our use of the past tense. Most Methodists today find Wesley's stress on "entire sanctification" puzzling, something from another world, for at least two reasons. First, Wesleyan sanctification is from another time and place; the language Wesley used to describe holiness seems foreign to us. Second, more significantly, Wesley made sanctification a work of the Holy Spirit. Wesley never expected anyone to "go on toward perfection" by himself or herself (even today United Methodist ministers are asked by the bishop, at their ordination, if they are "going on toward perfection"; then the bishop prays, "Come, Holy Spirit!").

The Holy Spirit is "from another world" because the Holy Spirit is God. Yet through the work of the Holy Spirit that "other world" turns out to be the same world in which we live and move and have our being (Acts 17:28). Through the Holy Spirit we are made participants in another world: the world of God's life as Trinity. The Holy Spirit validates that God is closer than we are to ourselves. Not only is this true, but by the grace of God we are transformed to be witnesses that through the work of the Holy Spirit God claims us as friends, citizens of the kingdom of Christ.

Neither of us can claim to be an exemplary Christian. We still have some distance to go on our way to "perfection." But trust us; you would not have wanted to know us before the Holy Spirit got hold of us.

Many holiness themes are now treated under the general category of *ethics*—by which is usually meant the art of making ourselves into better people. *Sanctification* is now associated with *spirituality*—attempts to be more spiritually adept. This separation of ethics from the work of the Holy Spirit is fraught with difficulties. Once our relation with God is relegated to spirituality, we no longer have to think about ethics as if God matters in human behavior.

HOLINESS DEMANDS THAT WHATEVER ELSE MAY BE SAID ABOUT THE WORK OF THE HOLY SPIRIT, AT THE VERY LEAST WHAT MUST BE SAID IS THAT WHO GOD IS AND WHAT GOD DOES MATTERS. THE PROPER TASK OF TRULY *CHRISTIAN* ETHICS IS TO DISPLAY HOW THE HOLY SPIRIT MAKES A DIFFERENCE FOR CHRISTIAN LIVING.

Ethics—the reflection upon the virtues, decisions, and behaviors required of Christians—must be practiced so that questions of the good and right cannot be divorced from our theological convictions about who God is, what God commands, and what God does in us in Jesus Christ. *Holiness demands that whatever else may be said about the work of the Holy Spirit, at the very least what must be said is that who God is and what God does matters.*

The proper task of truly *Christian* ethics is to display how the Holy Spirit makes a difference for Christian living.

It cannot be denied, however, that the language of holiness, or to use Wesley's language, *perfection*, sounds archaic if not pretentious. Most of us distrust people who might presume to be "perfect." Given our sinfulness, who has the gall to think he or she is holy? The characterization of someone as "holier than thou" is no compliment.

True, we are willing to think that someone like Mother Teresa was holy, though we are unsure what that means other than she must have been heroically good. People so unselfish we admire, but we also regard them as unique individuals whose lives most of us are not only incapable of living but really would not want to live. We admire Mother Teresa but would not want to have her as a friend.

Or would we? Rowan Williams observes that the coherence of the worldviews of some of the most significant thinkers in the Anglican tradition depended less on a theological system "than on a sense of what a human life looks like when it is in the process of being transformed by God in Christ. For them thinking about God was bound up with thinking about how human beings became holy, came to show in their lives the grace and glory of God."[7]

The point Williams makes not only is important but also makes clear that Charles and John Wesley's stress on Christian perfection, while perhaps distinctive in ways unique to them, was a theme deeply embedded in the prayers, liturgies, and theology of English theological tradition. The Catholic sense of holiness associated with the Eucharist and the Reformed emphasis on the sacralizing of everyday life were both present in the tradition of the Church of England and were of decisive influence on the Wesleys.

Williams does, however, identify a "reflective and theological scepticism"[8] that runs through the Anglican tradition concerning holiness. It is a skepticism that recognizes that we are fallen creatures whose outward signs of holiness will always be ambiguous. We are ever ready to deceive ourselves. Such skepticism about our ability to be holy, a skepticism to which Wesley may well have not paid sufficient attention, can paradoxically be regarded as a sign of holiness.[9] For it is surely the case, as the testimony of saints confirms, the nearer anyone draws to God the more likely he or she will be convicted of his or her sin.

IN SCRIPTURE HOLINESS IS NOT AN INDIVIDUAL ACHIEVEMENT BUT RATHER A COMMUNAL REFLECTION OF *GOD'S* GLORY AND HOLINESS.

It is very important—in order to understand better what holiness entails, or how best to reclaim the language of holiness as a way to describe our lives as Christians—to attend to scripture. In scripture holiness is not an individual achievement but rather a communal reflection of *God's* glory and holiness. God alone is holy; that is, God is God and we are not. Isaiah's vision in the temple is surely one of the most determinative expressions of what it means to confront God's sheer "otherness." Isaiah describes his encounter with God this way:

> In the year of King Uzziah's death, I saw the Lord sitting on a high and exalted throne, the edges of his robe filling the temple. Winged creatures were stationed around him. Each had six wings: with two they veiled their faces, with two their feet, and with two they flew about. They shouted to each other, saying:

> > "Holy, holy, holy is the LORD of heavenly forces!
> > All the earth is filled with God's glory!" (Isa 6:1-3)

Overwhelmed by God's glory, Isaiah confesses that he is a man of "unclean lips," making him a doubtful agent of such a God (Isa 6:5). But a seraph, taking a coal from the altar, touches Isaiah's lips, blotting out Isaiah's sins. Isaiah has been sanctified, made holy, and thereby prepared to perform his prophetic task. *To be holy is to be commandeered by God to perform a divine assignment.*

Set Apart by the Spirit

The prophet's task was to remind Israel that she is a people only because God had chosen her to be God's holy people. From the beginning God called Israel to be a people unlike any other. Abraham was called to walk blameless before God (Gen 17:1). He was to do so because he would be the father of a people whose very existence depended on being set apart as God's. To be set apart is not only what is necessary to be holy, but it is the very form that holiness must take if the nations of the world are to see the difference the holiness of God makes for us as God's creatures.

With Israel's exodus from Egypt, the connection between Israel being set apart and holiness became a dominant plot in the story of God and Israel. At Mount Sinai God had Moses say to the house of Jacob:

> You saw what I did to the Egyptians, and how I lifted you up on eagles' wings and brought you to me. So now, if you faithfully obey me and stay true to my covenant, you will be my most precious possession out of all the peoples, since the whole earth belongs to me. You will be a kingdom of priests

for me and a holy nation. These are the words you should say to the Israelites. (Exod 19:4-6)

Israel was given the Law that she might have the means to avoid idolatry. God had shown passionate, public commitment to Israel and did not mean to share Israel with any pretend god. Israel was called to be "a kingdom of priests" whose faithfulness to God would be seen by the other nations as what God could make of a sinful people. Israel's holiness was first of all a function of God's relationship to and plans for Israel.

Israel was accordingly separated from the practices of other people that would compromise her witness to the holiness of God. This is made explicit in Leviticus. God charged Moses to tell the whole congregation of the people of Israel that they "must be holy, because I, the LORD your God, am holy" (Lev 19:2). Just as God's holiness was manifest in God's care of Israel, so Israel must care for the alien, the poor, and the dispossessed as a reflection of God's holiness (Deut 10:19).

Particularly significant is the holiness of God's name. God is a jealous God who forbids the wrongful use of his name. Yet according to Ezekiel, that is exactly what Israel did. They profaned God's name by forsaking the land God had given them. It was a land, moreover, that was sacred in a manner that other lands were not. Though Israel betrayed God's promise, God refused to let Israel alone. God acted to save Israel for the sake of God's holy name. God sanctifies his name by gathering Israel from the nations. Accordingly Israel would be sprinkled with clean water, cleansed of all idolatry, and given a heart of flesh (Ezek 36:20-32).

71

This pattern of the Old Testament in which the people of God were called out to reflect God's glory is clearly on display in the New Testament:

> Therefore, once you have your minds ready for action and you are thinking clearly, place your hope completely on the grace that will be brought to you when Jesus Christ is revealed. Don't be conformed to your former desires, those that shaped you when you were ignorant. But, as obedient children, you must be holy in every aspect of your lives, just as the one who called you is holy. It is written, *You will be holy, because I am holy.* (1 Pet 1:13-16)

Peter charged those to whom he wrote to rid themselves of malice, guile, insincerity, envy, and slander. Just like Israel, once they were no people but now they were "a chosen race, a royal priesthood, a holy nation, a people who are God's own possession." They were people set apart to "speak of the wonderful acts of the one who called you out of darkness into his amazing light" (1 Pet 2:9).

Paul employed the same understanding of the relation of God's holiness to our reflection of that holiness in his first letter to the Thessalonians. He urged the Thessalonians to live lives pleasing to God. Such lives, lives of sanctification, meant that they were to abstain from fornication because followers of Christ must know how to control their own bodies. It is not so much that Christians must control their passions but rather that the passions have become ordered to ends that the Holy Spirit makes available.

Perhaps nothing is more indicative of the change being a Christian entails than Paul's command to the Thessalonians not to seek vengeance even if they thought they had been wronged. This is particularly important for the relations they had with their fellow brothers and sisters in Christ. Vengeance is God's. Life without vengeance is possible because God "didn't call us to be immoral but to be dedicated to him. Therefore, whoever rejects these instructions isn't rejecting a human authority. They are rejecting God, who gives his Holy Spirit to you" (1 Thess 4:7-8). *There is a direct correlation between the holiness of the Holy Spirit and the holiness that characterizes those who make up the church.*

Paul assumed that through baptism a new people had been called into existence to be for the world what Jesus was and continues to be—the manifestation of the reality of God's love. Once they were no people but now they are a holy people. To be a holy people does not mean the church is without sin. Indeed the holiness of the church as well as those who make it up depends on the recognition that they often fail to be what God has made them through baptism. But Jesus has offered those called to follow him participation through the Spirit in a community and way of life otherwise unimaginable, participants in the very life of the Trinity.

Once again, Romans 8 is helpful for understanding the role of the Spirit to create a holy people. Paul began by observing that the "law of the Spirit of life in Christ Jesus" has set them free "from the law of sin and death" (Rom 8:2). To set the mind on the flesh is to be orientated toward death, but they have been freed from that captivity through the Spirit setting their minds on life and peace (Rom 8:6). According to Paul, if the Spirit of him who raised Jesus from the dead is in us, life will be given to our mortal bodies through the Spirit that dwells in us. Through the Spirit we have been made children of God, heirs of Christ, and if we suffer with him, we will be glorified with him (Rom 8:11-17).

PRAYER IS THE CRUCIAL PRACTICE THROUGH WHICH WE ARE DRAWN INTO THE LIFE OF THE TRINITY.

Prayer is the crucial practice through which we are drawn into the life of the Trinity. All creation has been groaning in labor pains waiting for the Spirit. That same groaning pervades our attempts at prayer. Since we don't know how to pray as we should, the Spirit "intercedes with sighs too deep for words" (Rom 8:26 NRSV). Those sighs are intercession for God to have the Spirit intercede for us. Sarah Coakley observes that Paul's understanding of *the Spirit's role in making our prayers God's prayers means we, and indeed all creation, are actually caught up into the life of God.*[10] To be so "caught" is to be made holy.

The Spirit of Friendship

The relationship between prayer and holiness is at the heart of Jesus's farewell discourses in the Gospel of John. Jesus tells his disciples that he will be betrayed and killed. He will, therefore, be with them only a little longer. But they are not to be dismayed. Since he is going to the Father, Jesus will pray that the advocate be sent, who will be with them forever. That advocate is the "Spirit of Truth" whom the world cannot know but the disciples will recognize because the Holy Spirit abides in them (John 14:17). The truth that the advocate, who is the Holy Spirit, will remind the disciples is that which Jesus has taught—to love one another as he has loved them (John 14:25-31).

That Jesus commands the disciples to love one another is an indication that love is not some general disposition that we possess whether Jesus loves us or not. Rather Jesus commanded them to love one another *as he loved them*. His love for his disciples ended on a cross. This is a love that is likely to lead to death because it is a love that refuses to let death determine the limits or the boldness of our love of God and one another. That Jesus commands his disciples to love one another is a challenge to all sentimental accounts of love that presume loving another risks no loss. Friendship becomes the risky but blessed playground of the Spirit's work.

The advocate, therefore, is the agent who makes a friendship possible between Jesus and his disciples, friendship that is the mark of holiness (John 15:12-17). John's Gospel is noted for its emphasis upon the community of Christ and the ethics demanded to be in community with one another (the church) in Christ's name. For instance, Jesus makes no commandment to love enemies, as Jesus does in Matthew. Jesus in John's Gospel seems to think that the way Christians love the world is by loving one another in the church, showing the world the new way of life that is possible under the compulsion of the Holy Spirit.

John's Gospel therefore shows a decidedly "in-house" ethics. We ought not to be embarrassed by this communitarian focus. It's a great challenge to love in church. All of us know that it's easier to love our neighbors in the abstract, those who are far away, than to love people with whom we must intimately work and pray within the Christian community. The church shows that the Holy Spirit, the spirit of truth, constitutes a relation between people otherwise unimaginable exactly because it is a *friendship based on truth*. Such a friendship is necessary because, as Jesus tells the disciples, the time is coming when they will also face death from those who think they are doing God's will. They will discover they will need the bond of friendship the advocate provides, as they must learn to live in a world that knows not Jesus (John 16:4-11).

In the next chapter we will attend more closely to Jesus's farewell discourses in the Gospel of John. We call attention to them now because they provide a way to think about holiness that avoids the danger of sanctimoniousness. *To be made holy by the work of the Holy Spirit is to be made part of a community of truth that makes friendship possible in a world of violence and lies.* We are violent because of the lies we tell one another in our desperate attempts to force others to love us. To be sanctified is to be made a participant in a way of life through which we discover friends who tell us the truth.

TO BE MADE HOLY BY THE WORK OF THE HOLY SPIRIT IS TO BE MADE PART OF A COMMUNITY OF TRUTH THAT MAKES FRIENDSHIP POSSIBLE IN A WORLD OF VIOLENCE AND LIES.

Again we say that holiness is not a popular way to understand what it means to be a Christian. By directing attention to the interrelation of the "Spirit of Truth" and friendship, we hope to suggest a way to understand the kind of holiness that is at the heart of the work of the Holy Spirit. To be holy is not to be morally better than anyone we know; to be holy is to be made part of a community in which our lives depend on those we know and who know us. To be made holy is to be held accountable and to hold others accountable, to be loved and to love as we have been loved by Christ, the one who would have us love one another even if such love invites the hatred of the world.

In his letter to the Ephesians, Paul commands the Ephesians not to steal, not to let "any foul words come out of your mouth" (Eph 4:29), and to avoid obscene, silly, and vulgar talk (Eph 4:17-32). The temptation is to think of these recommendations as a list that constitutes what one must do to be holy or at least morally good. But that makes holiness into a moralistic program or a set of ideals that is hard to attain, but one must nonetheless try hard to do so. What is lost in such trying is the dependence on the work of the Holy Spirit to forge friendships

77

that make it possible for us to live lives of truth in a world of lies.

To be sure fornication, stealing, or "foul words" are not to be done by Christians, but the reason such behaviors are forbidden is that they are behaviors that destroy community by making it difficult for people to trust one another. Mistrust kills friendship. To be holy does not mean moral perfection. Rather, holiness is the work of the Holy Spirit that makes us participants in the perfect love that constitutes the relation between the persons of the Trinity.

Wesley's language of perfection can give the impression that if you are "perfect" your life has come to a stop; you are done. That's not what Wesley thought. For Wesley perfection was a journey that was never complete in this life. Because perfection is a journey in love, we need all the friends we can get to sustain us on the way. In his history of spirituality, Robert Davis Hughes III observes that if we are to grow as we must, if we are to unlearn hate and learn to love, our flesh must be disciplined not because it is evil, though it often tempts us to sin, but because our flesh is us. Our embodied life of spirited dust is who we are. The Holy Spirit shapes us to be friends of Jesus by shaping our bodies with virtues that come from graced practices.[11]

Hughes, drawing on Wesley, observes that from a Christian point of view a *spirituality that does not entail growth in virtue, and in particular growth in the active love of neighbor, cannot be the work of the Holy Spirit.* The virtues are the necessary habits that help us along the way exactly because the Christian life is a journey we cannot attain by ourselves. The theological virtues of faith, hope, and love co-inhere just as the persons of the Trinity relate to one another. We learn to trust because God is faithful, hope is born of a humility sparked by the joy engendered by worship of God, and love is the shaping of our desires by God's unrelenting graceful presence.[12]

According to Hughes, joy is the unmistakable indication of a life of holiness shaped by the Holy Spirit. Joy can be distinguished from happiness only because joy abides even in circumstances that may threaten life. Hughes drives this point home by suggesting that true joy is rightly associated with the Christian virtues of martyrdom because true martyrs never lay a guilt trip on those who persecute them. Martyrs "quietly go on developing a virtuous character even in the face of adversity." Christian joy abides by keeping the commandment to love, by enjoying being the friend of Jesus even to share in his sorrow, which will finally be transformed into joy.[13]

The Spirit's Home

Spirit-induced holiness and Spirit-filled joy tend to complement one another. That's why holiness looks like a L'Arche home where assistants live with core members of the home. The core members are people with a wide variety of mental limits. We have been in such homes and can testify to the joy that pervades the very air in these places.

L'Arche was the creation of an extraordinary man named Jean Vanier. Vanier is a Canadian who had volunteered to be in the navy in World War II. After the war he felt lost. A French priest told him to take care of two older men who were suffering from different kinds of disability. Thus begins the story of L'Arche, the establishment of homes around the world for the mentally handicapped that ensure they will receive adequate care but, just as important, that they will claim others as friends and be claimed as friends.

In his commentary on the Gospel of John, *Drawn into the Mystery of Jesus through the Gospel of John*, Vanier comments on the sending of the advocate, the Paraclete, in John 14. He observes that the Paraclete "is given to those who are lonely and in need of a friend, to those who are lost and poor in spirit and who cry out to God."[14] He comments that the Holy Spirit gives us strength, which is nothing but love, to do the works of God by giving us friends who can help us do what we have been called to do.

Vanier notes that Jesus gives us commandments that we are to keep so the Paraclete will be given to us. They are, however, essentially commandments of love. We are to serve one another, to be in communion with one another, not to judge or condemn but always to be ready to forgive. We are to wash one another's feet, a key commandment for Vanier, who has often described how important it is to have one's feet washed by a core member. That practice and all the commandments are designed to form us into a people ready to receive the Holy Spirit who will live in the church and also be at home in each person of the church.[15]

THE HOLY SPIRIT GIVES US STRENGTH, WHICH IS NOTHING BUT LOVE, TO DO THE WORKS OF GOD BY GIVING US FRIENDS WHO CAN HELP US DO WHAT WE HAVE BEEN CALLED TO DO.

Stanley witnessed holiness in action at L'Arche:

I have seen the work of the Holy Spirit in L'Arche on a visit with Jean Vanier and his community of friends in France. On a Sunday I saw holiness enacted. The "church" was a converted barn. The mass was in the late afternoon. The congregation gathered slowly; many were in wheelchairs. A number of core members helped other core members find seats on the simple benches. The mass began with core members assisting by lighting candles, carrying the cross and Scripture. One young woman danced around the altar. The priest did what priests do in a manner that made clear he rejoiced in what was happening around him.

Just as the mass was beginning, Jean came in pushing an elderly core member in her wheelchair. He parked at the end of one of the lower benches and sat beside her. She leaned her head on his shoulder and did not move from that position until it came time to receive the body and blood of Christ. I have never seen a more gentle gesture. She and Jean had all the time in the world to be present to one another as the Holy Spirit was making Christ present in word and sacrament. I am sure that I caught a glimpse of heaven and the communion of the saints in that moment. The Spirit had come to rest on the body in a manner that was unmistakable.

Vanier observes that the body of Jesus is the dwelling place of God; Jesus is the new temple. But as Jesus and the Father come to dwell in us, *we* become the temple of God, the place where God lives. *We as church—that is, the assembly of believers—but also we as individuals become a habitation for the Spirit.* That is why Paul says to the Corinthians, "Do you not know that your body is a temple of the Holy Spirit?" (1 Cor 6:19 NRSV).

Before he leaves, Jesus tells his disciples that he is leaving them his peace, but he does so not as the world gives peace. The world tries to establish peace through half-truths, power plays, and coercion, but the peace that the Holy Spirit enacts is not the bogus order secured by violence that so many call "peace." The peace of Christ comes through the work of the Holy Spirit, whose task of always pointing us to Jesus makes possible a disavowal of violence and in such a disavowal the birth of friendship.

A pastor was appointed to an all-white church and to an all-black church located barely a mile from one another. The bishop told him that it was his task to try to bring the two congregations together.

"I was terrified. I knew that to attempt something this holy, this demanding, I would fail without the constant, miraculous intervention of the Holy Spirit." Every morning and evening the pastor prayed earnestly for the visitation, empowerment, and guidance of the Spirit. He taught his congregations, at every turn in the road, before every decision and each new move, to pray in effect, "Holy Spirit, if you want us to be one church, you must walk with us."

Three years later the Holy Spirit has produced one of the few truly multiracial congregations in that part of the world.

"Come, Holy Spirit!"

Chapter Four

LAST THINGS

hristianity is a historical reality. The historic reality of Christianity is not just that the church has a history, but rather
that our God actually showed up in history. God, thank
God, refuses to leave the course of human history up to us humans alone. *Even as the Holy Spirit takes up space by resting upon
bodies, so the Holy Spirit is the typical, continuing way that the
Trinity is made known in time.* If we want to know God, we need
not float up into some detached spiritual Never-Never Land.
God, in the Holy Spirit, has come to us, met us, right now, right
here. God is not some transcendental idea, but rather God is
known through witnesses across time. We believe those witnesses
have been called into existence and made to witness through the
work of the Holy Spirit. Even more remarkable, we believe that
through the Holy Spirit we are drawn into the very life of God
through the mediation of God's Son, Jesus Christ. The name
given that reality is the *kingdom of God*, which we believe is anticipated in the church.

Christians are an eschatological people. *Eschatology* means
we are a people of time who in this time have seen in Christ
the end time. Eschatology is the Christian doctrine dealing
with "last things." For Christians the end has always been in

the beginning. We were created to be creatures whose end *telos* (purpose) and end (destination) is God. Accordingly our time as an eschatological people is a different time from the world's time because God has taken time for us. Our time is the time that the Holy Spirit makes possible because the Holy Spirit is the agent of the kingdom inaugurated by Christ. That is why the Christian new year is called *Advent*, that time when God comes to us, making our history with God possible.

WE WERE CREATED TO BE CREATURES WHOSE END *TELOS* (PURPOSE) AND END (DESTINATION) IS GOD. OUR FINAL END IS ETERNAL WORSHIP OF GOD.

We do not, therefore, believe that the time in which we live, a time called *history*, is without meaning. Our lives are not pointless, one thing after another, random luck headed nowhere. We are created for the glory of God, which is enacted now in our worship of God. Our final end is eternal worship of God. In Sunday morning worship we are drawn into the narrative of God's care of creation and salvation of all through the calling of Israel to be his people and the engrafting of Gentiles to Israel through Jesus of Nazareth. All of which means that *through the Holy Spirit we exchange our citizenship in this age and are made citizens of the new age.*

It is not accidental, therefore, that the Nicene Creed ends with our acknowledgment of "one baptism for the forgiveness of sins," an affirmation of our expectation of "the resurrection of the dead," and "hope for life in the world to come." Those are realities that the Holy Spirit makes integral to our lives as Christians, now. We already share in the life that is to come because the Holy Spirit has rested on our bodies in baptism. Through baptism we are made citizens of a new community that must be an alternative to the world. Eternal life, life with God, does not wait until the end of our lives.

Throughout our discussion of the Holy Spirit we have returned to Paul's account of the Spirit in Romans 8, a decisive eschatological text. Paul admits that death threatens, but death has been defeated through Christ. "If the Spirit of the one who raised Jesus from the dead lives in you, the one who raised Christ from the dead will give life to your human bodies also, through his Spirit that lives in you" (Rom 8:11). Romans 8 accordingly ends with the ringing affirmation in which Paul expresses his deepest conviction that "nothing can separate us from God's love in Christ Jesus our Lord: not death or life, not angels or rulers, not present things or future things, not powers, or height or depth, or any other thing that is created" (Rom 8:38-39).

Paul's affirmation of the defeat of death finds expression in our baptism liturgy when we pray: "We thank you, Father, for the water of Baptism. In it we are buried with Christ in his death. By it we share in his resurrection. Through it we are reborn by the Holy Spirit. Therefore in joyful obedience to your Son, we bring into his fellowship those who come to him in faith, baptizing them in the Name of the Father, of the Son, and of the Holy Spirit."[1] This is not just pious language meant to hide from us the reality of death. Rather, it is our most realistic language about the Holy Spirit, who makes us share in Christ's victory over death.

Our last, best hope in death is the same hope that we bear in life: that the God who has so relentlessly pursued us, who saves us in Christ's work for us, who draws us into the fellowship of his cross and resurrection, will continue to pursue us, save us, draw us near even in our deaths.

Stanley is a communicant in a congregation whose baptistery is in the form of a large cross making possible baptism by immersion. To be under the water in baptism intimates our death because we are unable to breathe. Paul's major image for baptism is death (Rom 6:3-4). In baptism we are reborn, re-created, gifted but not without our sinful selves being put to death so that we might rise to the life God intends for us. Something is gained in our entrance into the Christian life but something is also lost, and the loss (repentance) may be painful. Baptism signifies all of the mystery that is our death/rebirth in God's saving work in us.

Under the guidance of the Holy Spirit, Stanley's church has determined that when a member of the congregation dies, the body is brought to the church the day before the funeral and the coffin is placed on the baptistery. Members of the church then stay with the body through the day and night before the funeral. This liturgical action gives concrete expression to their conviction that death has not defeated us. Even as God brought us through the waters of baptism to life in Christ, so shall we be brought through the waters of death. Through the Spirit we have been made part of God's end time.

This liturgical action is a sign of what it means to be a community who has learned to live in anticipation of life in the world to come. John Wesley used to brag, "Our people die well." Baptism into Christ is dress rehearsal for our dying. Because a new world has been made present through the Spirit, we believe we are a people of a new age even though the old age continues. When the church embraces a sister or brother in baptism, receiving into God's family one of God's own, laying on the newly baptized the designation *Christian*, we are being given a glimpse, a reassurance of what God intends for all, what God will do in fullness at the end of our time. We are a people who live in two times. We believe that the Holy Spirit makes us members of a new age in which sin no longer reigns because we have been made a people whose sins have been forgiven. Accordingly we are no longer haunted by death or jerked around by a suffocating fear of death. We can breathe.

To be sure, the Christian sense of the end puts us in tension with the world. We live in a world too often determined by the denial of death. Christians are a people who, under the guidance of the Spirit, know how to be honest about death and how to be present to one another in death. Eschatology challenges all politics based on the illusion that we can somehow get out of life alive, that we can secure our lives by ourselves. *Church* is the name for a people who challenge the presumption that we live in a world in which some must die so that others may live secure.

IS CHURCH POSSIBLE? ONLY FOR THOSE WHO ARE BOLD TO PRAY, "COME, HOLY SPIRIT!"

World names all those who have attempted to live as if their lives are their own, as if this time is under our control, as if we can secure ourselves through the power of the state, military might, or other human means, and who refuse to believe that Christ is the end of time. *Church* names that radical political alternative where Christians learn to live as people who refuse to let the politics of death determine our lives. Our desire as Christians is to live with the sort of nonviolent patience and courage that make no sense to the world if God is not Father, Son, and Holy Spirit. We want more than anything to live in such a way that the world has no sociological, anthropological, gender-related, racial, economic explanation for us other than we are a people who have been given what they prayed for: "Come, Holy Spirit."

A long time ago we teamed up to write *Resident Aliens: Life in the Christian Colony*. We called a dying church to see itself as God's peculiar answer to what is wrong with the world. We urged the church to be that countercultural reality that is an alternative to the world's ways of organizing people. We pleaded for Christians to stand together against the wiles of the world, the seductions of this economy, and the lies that bolster the modern nation state.

While we suggested some alternative ways of being the church and urged a recovery of the church's ancient practices and self-understandings, even though we gave some examples of contemporary churches embodying the vision of God's "colony of heaven" in an often heartless world (Phil 3:20-21), looking back we wish we had more strongly asserted one thing. Courageous Christian witness, daily determination by the love of Christ rather than the competing loves of the world, non-violent testimony in a death-dealing world at war, true and vibrant worship—is church possible?

Only for those who are bold to pray, "Come, Holy Spirit!"

THE CREEDS

The Nicene Creed

We believe in one God,
    the Father, the Almighty,
    maker of heaven and earth,
    of all that is, seen and unseen.

We believe in one Lord, Jesus Christ,
    the only Son of God,
    eternally begotten of the Father,
    God from God, Light from Light,
    true God from true God,
    begotten, not made,
    of one Being with the Father;
    through him all things were made.
    For us and for our salvation,
        he came down from heaven,
        was incarnate of the Holy Spirit and the Virgin
        Mary
        and became truly human.
        For our sake he was crucified under Pontius Pilate;
        he suffered death and was buried.

On the third day he rose again
in accordance with the Scriptures;
he ascended into heaven
and is seated at the right hand of the Father.
He will come again in glory
to judge the living and the dead,
and his kingdom will have no end.

We believe in the Holy Spirit, the Lord, the giver of life,
who proceeds from the Father and the Son,
who with the Father and the Son
is worshiped and glorified,
who has spoken through the prophets.
We believe in the one holy catholic and apostolic
church.
We acknowledge baptism
for the forgiveness of sins.
We look for the resurrection of the dead,
and the life of the world to come. Amen.

The Apostles' Creed

I believe in God, the Father Almighty,
creator of heaven and earth.

I believe in Jesus Christ, his only Son, our Lord,
who was conceived by the Holy Spirit,
born of the Virgin Mary,
suffered under Pontius Pilate,
was crucified, died, and was buried;
he descended to the dead.
On the third day he rose again;

he ascended into heaven,
is seated at the right hand of the Father,
and will come again to judge the living and the dead.

I believe in the Holy Spirit,
    the holy catholic church,
    the communion of saints,
    the forgiveness of sins,
    the resurrection of the body
    and the life everlasting. Amen.

NOTES

Introduction

1. Stanley Hauerwas and William Willimon, *Resident Aliens: Life in the Christian Colony*, rev. ed. (Nashville: Abingdon, 2014).

1. Trinity

1. See Jason Byassee's book in the Belief Matters series, *Trinity: The God We Don't Know* (Nashville: Abingdon, 2015).

2. H. E. W. Turner, *The Pattern of Christian Truth* (London: Mowbray, 1954), 35.

3. This is Eugene Rogers's formulation of the question in his book *After the Spirit: A Constructive Pneumatology from Resources outside the Modern West* (Grand Rapids: Eerdmans, 2005), 19.

4. Robert W. Jenson, *Systematic Theology*, vol. 1, *The Triune God* (New York: Oxford, 1997), 36.

5. Rogers, *After the Spirit*, 14.

6. Ibid., 7.

7. Quoted in ibid., 56.

8. Ibid., 174.

9. Sarah Coakley, *God, Sexuality, and the Self: An Essay "On the Trinity"* (Cambridge: Cambridge University Press, 2013), 101.

10. Ibid., 112–13.

11. "The Holy Eucharist: Rite I," in *The Book of Common Prayer* (New York: Church Publishing, 2007), 334.

12. Karl Rahner, *The Trinity* (London: Continuum, 2001).

13. John D. Zizioulas, *Being as Communion: Studies in Person-hood and the Church* (New York: St. Vladmir's Seminary, 1997), 17.

14. Ibid., 110–11.

15. "The Baptismal Covenant I," in *The United Methodist Hymnal* (Nashville: The United Methodist Publishing House, 1989), 36. Used by permission of Abingdon Press, all rights reserved.

16. "A Service of Word and Table I," in *The United Methodist Hymnal* (Nashville: The United Methodist Publishing House, 1989), 6.

17. *The Book of Common Prayer* (New York: Church Publishing, 2007), 363.

18. Augustine, *Homilies on the First Epistle of John*, trans. Boniface Ramsey (New York: New City, 2008), 108.

2. Pentecost

1. Nicholas Lash, *Believing Three Ways in One God: A Reading of the Apostles' Creed* (South Bend, IN: University of Notre Dame Press, 1993), 87.

2. Claude Welch, *The Reality of the Church* (New York: Scribner's Sons, 1998), 223.

3. Ibid.

4. The names in this story have been changed.

5. See Will's book in the Belief Matters series, *Incarnation: The Surprising Overlap of Heaven and Earth* (Nashville: Abingdon, 2013).

6. Stephen Pickard, *Seeking the Church: An Introduction to Ecclesiology* (London: SCM Press, 2012), 59–60.

7. Ibid., 63.

8. Ibid., 62.

9. Ibid., 224.

10. Ibid., 216.

11. Rowan Williams, *Tokens of Trust: An Introduction to Christian Belief* (Louisville: Westminster John Knox, 2007), 105.

12. Lash, *Believing Three Ways in One God*, 85.

13. We are indebted to Claude Welch for these references to scripture to describe the work of the Spirit for the upbuilding of the church. See his book *The Reality of the Church*, 218.

14. Ibid., 214.

15. James F. Kay, *Preaching and Theology* (St. Louis, MO: Chalice, 2007), 132.

16. C. Kavin Rowe, *World Upside Down: Reading Acts in the Graeco-Roman Age* (Oxford: Oxford University Press, 2009), 120.

17. Welch, *The Reality of the Church,* 240.

18. Williams, *Tokens of Trust*, 128.

19. Ibid., 129.

20. Welch, *The Reality of the Church*, 126.

3. Holiness

1. Charles Wesley, "Love Divine, All Loves Excelling," in *The United Methodist Hymnal* (Nashville: The United Methodist Publishing House, 1989), 384.

2. John Wesley, "Christian Perfection," in *John Wesley*, ed. Albert Outler (New York: Oxford University Press, 1980), 253.

3. John Wesley, "Thoughts on Christian Perfection," Q 25, in *Doctrinal and Controversial Treatises II*, ed. Paul Wesley Chilcote and Kenneth J. Collins, vol. 13 of *The Bicentennial Edition of the Works of John Wesley* (Nashville: Abingdon, 2013), 73.

4. Wesley, "Christian Perfection," in Outler, *John Wesley*, 293.

5. John Wesley, "The Fullness of Faith," in Outler, *John Wesley*, 274.

6. Ibid., 275.

7. Rowan Williams, "Introduction," in *Love's Redeeming Work: The Anglican Quest for Holiness*, comp. Geoffrey Rowell, Kenneth Stevenson, and Rowan Williams (Oxford: Oxford University Press, 2001), xxiv.

8. Ibid., xxi.

9. Ibid., xxv.

10. Sarah Coakley, *God, Sexuality, and the Self: An Essay "On the Trinity"* (Cambridge: Cambridge University Press, 2013), 111.

11. Robert Davis Hughes III, *Beloved Dust: Tides of the Spirit in the Christian Life* (New York: Continuum, 2011), 126–27.

12. Ibid., 131–49.

13. Ibid.

14. Jean Vanier, *Drawn into the Mystery of Jesus through the Gospel of John* (New York: Paulist, 2004), 260.

15. Ibid., 262–63.

4. Last Things

1. "Holy Baptism," in *The Book of Common Prayer* (New York: Church Publishing, 2007), 306–7.

Lightning Source UK Ltd.
Milton Keynes UK
UKOW04f1123141015

260512UK00003B/39/P